Chasing Tuna

The Beginner's Guide to West Coast Offshore Fishing

By Matt Steiger

©2016, Matt Steiger, All rights reserved

Table of Contents

Chasing Tuna

- **Chapter 1: Offshore Fishing** 1
    - Who am I? 4
    - Why fish? 5
    - The Fisheries 8
- **Chapter 2: Planning Your Trip** 37
    - The Trips 37
    - The Landing 41
    - The Landing Count 41
    - The Season 44
    - The Boat 47
- **Chapter 3: Gearing Up** 49
    - Rods 49
    - Reels 51
    - Rod & Reel Combos 54
    - To Buy or Lease 58
    - Line Choice and Drag 59
    - Terminal Tackle 61
    - Lures 64
    - Knots 67
    - Other Gear 68
    - Clothing, sun protection, and footwear 69
- **Chapter 4: Get Onboard** 70
    - Packing and Parking 70
    - Find your bunk 70
    - Signing in 72
    - Food and drink 74
    - Seasickness 76
- **Chapter 5: Get Fishing!** 80
    - Basic Fishing 80
    - Advanced Fishing Topics 92
    - The Fight 95
    - Key Fishing Concepts Summary 100

iii

Chapter 6: Handling the Catch..101
    Fish Cleaning..101
    Processing and Storage...103
    Cooking and eating 106
About the Author 116

Chapter 1: Offshore Fishing

There was a deathly calm over the whole boat as we drifted past the kelp paddy. After a day of trolling and searching, we had finally found a huge floating mass of seaweed and its promise of hidden fish. Offshore fishing is marked by long periods of uncomfortable waiting – nowhere to sit, sun beating down, boat rocking in the tide – interrupted by brief flurries of activity.

....

An experienced angler knows the telltale signs of a prospect. Sometimes the boat revs up and makes a dramatic 90-degree turn. Other times it's subtler: a slight shift of course or an almost imperceptible change in rpm's.

The latter usually marks a kelp paddy; a floating object in the vast nothingness. If you were to swim across the ocean you would most likely only see clear blue water. There is a marked lack of anything out there. But if you search hard, with a bit of luck, you might find some floating trash or perhaps a true oasis of the blue desert, a paddy.

In that expanse, teeny fish wander frantically looking for some sort of cover. The floating kelp provides shade, camouflage, even food as they eat the kelp itself and the bugs living in it. Bigger fish are also wandering the seas, looking for food. To them the kelp is a hunting ground. They gravitate toward the kelp as a focal point of the ocean.

To a fisherman the kelp is promise itself.

Our boat revved down and the captain came on the PA. "We got a kelp pad coming up, port side. Pull in the troll lines." The bait tank became the temporary center of our solar system; all anglers crowded around.

It's a matter of timing. The first baits in the water often get bit, so it pays to be ready to pitch in. But if you grab a bait too soon it will die in your hand, gasping for air. The bait tank has its own social dynamic. It only has room for about 4 anglers. Those lucky, or aggressive few stand guard; waiting to grab a bait and pin it on. The rest of us wait for our chance to elbow in.

The boat stops, baits are thrown, and suddenly the water's surface explodes with activity. Tuna are busting bait everywhere right on top. "BOIL!" scream the deck hands as they throw bait after bait into the open maw of a school of tuna.

Lines are cast, fish are hooked, and within minutes the whole boat is a raucous mess. Fish flop on the deck, blood splatters everywhere, fishermen struggle for position at the rail or work to untangle line, others push through to get a new bait and reset on the fishing.

The flurry of a school of tuna is an excitement little known in regular life. The sun bakes your face, the beads of sweat roll down your brow, your throat becomes parched, and blood is flying everywhere.

If you do hook a fish you're in for a surprisingly exhausting 15-20 minutes. On my first offshore fish, a 30 lb albacore, I almost puked from the exertion. With your fish landed you feel at once excited, relieved, sad for the kill, exhausted, and then…desperate to get another bait in the water.

On a good day this goes on for hours. There are stories of boats hitting a school in the morning and fishing it until they've reached their limit. Then handing it off to another boat.

More likely the flurry is woefully short lived. As quickly as it turned on, it can switch off. Suddenly all lines are slack, the wind even seems to die. The deck is hosed off, fish are put away, and it's as if everyone has been out for a pleasure cruise all afternoon.

....

We hit this paddy after a long day of searching. Rough seas, high winds, and gray sky make paddies almost impossible to see. But the late afternoon brought calmer weather and bluer skies. Suddenly the wind lay down, the ocean opened up, and the telltale dark brown of the kelp began to reveal itself to us.

The bite went off for a good hour; everyone landed a tuna or two. It was almost certainly the last paddy of what had been a productive but tough day. But now the flurry was over. There was nothing, just quiet.

I hooked on a new sardine and headed to the bow. I dropped him in the water where he sat confused for a moment, then suddenly torpedoed out into the vast blue freedom before him. I gently thumbed the reel. The two of us were connected. Figuratively, stranded together in the expanse of the great wet desert. Also literally, connected by a gossamer thread: 350 yards of 20 lb test monofilament. Up in the bow of the boat, away from the crowds and protective shade of the wheelhouse, I felt the sun baking my neck. Drops of sweat collected on my temple and slowly rolled down to my chin.

The quiet persisted on and on, building tension. Ever so slightly, the calm began to give way to the subtle buzz of the Captain and deckhands, growing restless on the bite-less drift. I began to sense that they were moments away from calling, "Reel 'em in boys, let's move out!" When suddenly my line began peeling out; ripping, ripping, ripping. I took a breath, counted, "one…twooo…threeeeee." I flipped the reel in gear, the line went taught. A metallic blue-green dorado burst from the water, 100 yards out. "HOOK UPPPP!!!!"

I was into the most thrilling fight I've ever had. The whole boat sat and watched, listless and agape, as I reeled in that fish. He leapt over and over and over, each time showing off his iridescence. The captain himself gaffed the fish for me, and on the way to the kill box, stopped to take a photo. Then suddenly, it was like someone had flipped the switch: the bite was ON. Everyone got bit, and the boat exploded in a new flurry of excited yells, tangled lines, and flopping fish.

Who am I?

My name is Matt, and I'm a fishaholic. I have been fishing my whole life, as probably, have you. I love it. For years I dreamed of "deep-sea fishing", but never knew how to break into it. It seemed expensive, exotic, and maybe something you did once in your life.

Late in life, my mother married into a saltwater family. My step-grandfather was an old San Diego tuna captain and his sons (one, my step-father) were veteran fisherman. When my stepbrother grew, he became a tuna captain himself, operating out of Cabo San Lucas.

Slowly, with their help (and some coin) I broke into offshore angling. I struggled at first, but quickly learned the secrets of hooking the big ones. Now everyone I know asks me how to get into deep sea fishing, so I decided to write it all down in a book.

In truth offshore fishing is fun and easy to get into. A whole system is in place to help you. Like most things in life, many of the obstacles disappear with proper application of money.

With a little guidance it's possible to get offshore quickly; probably tomorrow! And without breaking the bank. With skill, it's even possible to make your money back in meat.

I am by no means an expert fisherman. I'm not a guide, or even a professional sport. I'm a regular guy, who works a regular 9-6 job. If I'm lucky I might get to fool around on a pond, or in the bay, once every week or two.

But I never miss the offshore season. I always make at least one trip per year, and sometimes 2-3. The average deck hand knows 1,000x more about fishing than I do, and indeed I learn something new on every trip.

However I am a decent fisherman. With the system I will outline here, I am able to consistently out-catch not only the boat average, but usually almost everyone on board. On my last trip, of 36 anglers, 45 Bluefin tuna were landed; I was responsible for 9, including one more than twice the size of everyone else's. On the previous trip I managed to reel in 15 Bluefin before most people had even got out of bed.

On those trips, everyone begins to resent me. They sit there wondering why I'm catching all the fish. Sometimes I even stop catching fish to help and give advice, but people rarely want to hear it. But if you're reading this book, it's because you want to catch fish. And if you take my advice, you can. It's not hard; in fact it's dead simple. But it can seem opaque to the uninitiated.

What follows is not the guidance of an expert angler, but rather a primer for those wanting to get into the sport. This book will guide you through the fish, the season, the boat, the gear, and the fishing. I am going to tell you the few killer secrets I know, and then you'll be catching fish too. I'll also tell you what to do once you succeed; you're going to be bringing home an awful lot of fish.

One last thing before we begin: don't call it deep sea fishing, no one knows what that is. Call it offshore angling.

Why fish?

When most people think about fishing, they picture sitting in a chair by the lake, soaking a worm, and drinking a beer. In a word: boring. I'm sure fishing *would* be boring for people who don't know how to do it.

I've already told you that offshore fishing can have intense periods of waiting, sandwiching brief flurries of frenetic (Robin Williams in the '80s style) excitement. But for people who love to fish, *every* moment with a line in the water is electrifying. There is deathly calm that you know could be destroyed in an instant. When that moment comes, you will be engaging in a life-or-death struggle with a wild animal and possibly bringing home some food.

For me, and most people reading this book, fishing is a way of life. It is how we connect to the natural world. Whether that's by a stream or lake, or floating about in the ocean, it's a means to get outside, see some wildlife, and enjoy the world outside of a cubicle.

Nearly every time I step outside, I see some wonder of nature: plants, animals, and strange weather patterns. The world outside is awe-inspiring. Out at sea, you are bound to run into a plethora of sea life.

I can't recall a trip offshore where I didn't see dolphins. Usually it's just half a dozen messing around. They gravitate toward the boat and ride the cushion of water at the front, called a bow-wave. But sometimes the boat will stumble upon a super-pod, containing hundreds or even thousands of dolphins, of all types, sizes, and ages. Imagine as far as you can see, in every direction, thousands of dolphins leaping and playing. I have seen it.

The same baitfish that attract tuna and dolphins can also attract a variety of other sea life. Marlin thrash bait on the surface. Whales breach, open-mouthed, to engulf whole schools of baitfish. Sharks and sunfish and every sea bird you can think of abound. I have seen it.

At sea there are man-made wonders as well: Mexican purse seiners, scooping up entire schools of Bluefin tuna; an amazing and horrifying vision. Massive Navy hovercraft, 10's of miles from shore; helicopter, jet, and carrier operations; submarines breaching for a view. And shipping containers so large they could fit thousands of our small fishing craft just on their deck. I have seen it.

On one recent trip we came across a teeny tugboat towing an enormous decommissioned aircraft carrier. It was an amazing sight: a little dinghy, tethered to perhaps the largest floating vessel I've ever seen, by a chain that must have been 4-5' wide. The captain called over, and they said they were towing it around Cape Horn to Texas. It was too big to fit through the Panama Canal.

When you step out your front door there's no telling what adventure awaits you. And when you enter the natural world as a predator, as indeed every fisherman does, you enter with a keen awareness of life and death. When you go to the wilderness in search of meat, it's a much more visceral experience than a mere stroll or pleasure cruise; like the difference between going to the grocery store and looking at pictures of food.

When you hook a fish you can feel its strength through the line and rod. It struggles powerfully against death, but you must hang on if you want to eat. And when you finally land that fish, you watch with excitement and remorse as its life slips away. You are part of the ancient cycle of life and death; a dance in which we must all partake.

Let's not forget the primary purpose either. A successful fishing trip means fresh fish in the cooler: delicious, impeccably fresh, sushi grade fish to nourish your family and friends. Fishing is never guaranteed: weather, seasons, and even days vary. Sometimes, especially in the beginning, you might get skunked. But as you learn, you can really bring home the fish. If you are prepared to handle it, one offshore fishing excursion can keep you in fish for the rest of the year.

The Fisheries

There are a variety of species offshore in Southern California. Many resident species live here year-round, around the rocks, kelp forests, and islands. But we will focus on the fish that you can chase offshore. They follow warm water currents along the coast. These migratory (pelagic) species include tuna, yellowtail, wahoo, marlin, and opah.

This list is far from comprehensive, but it should contain the bulk of what you might see come over the rail; especially in Southern California. Alternative names, biological facts, and notes of flavor are included whenever possible.

This section also includes the state of each fishery. As anglers, we are on the front lines of species management (albeit, in the second row). It is in our own interest to make sure we are harvesting these fish in a sustainable way. It's irresponsible to keep more than we can use. And we must never take more than can be naturally replenished.

But take heart! As a sport fisherman you alone will not typically deplete the fishery. Hook and line is the most sustainable way to harvest fish, mainly because it is slow and difficult. We must a) find the fish, b) somehow convince them to bite, and then c) laboriously reel them in with an over-engineered coffee grinder. Hook and line is also favored because we can choose the exact size, number, and species of fish killed.

For state of the fishery, I consult both Fishwatch, from NOAA, and Seafood Watch, from Monterey Bay Aquarium. The latter even has a convenient phone app to help you on the go.

Fishing in Southern California means you might be in either Californian or Mexican waters. At present the limit in Mexico 10 fish, with no more than 5 of any species. Except that a shark or marlin counts as 5 fish and a dorado counts as 2.5 fish. In

California waters the limit is 10 fish total, of any combination. There are no size limits.

Please note that the regulations on Bluefin tuna have changed a lot over the past few years (2014-2016). Sometimes the fisheries have been closed altogether. As of summer 2016, the limit in both Mexico and California is 2 Bluefin tuna per angler. Make sure you Google it before you go, but the boats will be sure to let you know once you're out there.

Yellowfin Tuna - aka Yellowfin, YFT, ahi

Yellowfin tuna are extremely prolific in the Pacific. They grow quickly and breed often. These fish grow about 10 lb per year and will start spawning between the ages of three and five. It is said that a tuna can lay one million eggs a year, but only one of those will grow old enough to breed.

Tuna are nature's torpedoes. They are streamlined: tapered on both ends. They have a short, thin tail, which they can whip furiously around, achieving great speeds underwater. When someone on the boat lands a tuna you will hear the telltale whipping of its tail against the deck (dut-dut-dut-dut-dut-dut-dut). Like a playing card in a bicycle spoke, but much faster.

Tuna are a schooling fish. They travel in large groups of hundreds to thousands, especially when young. The schools follow dolphin around, looking for baitfish to eat. Often a school of tuna will work cooperatively with a pod of dolphins and/or a flock of birds. These three can demolish a school of 10,000 baitfish in a matter of minutes.

On the west coast we mainly encounter juvenile tuna. The typical size ranges from 20-30 lb. Sometimes we will find schools of fish in the 40-60 lb range, and those are exciting days. Rarely, a boat will hook and land a fish that weighs over one hundred pounds, but the big ones tend to stay around southern Mexico and Hawaii. Only in truly record-setting years, like 2015, do large numbers of huge fish move through our waters. But who knows, with changing weather patterns world-wide, perhaps this will be the new normal.

The tuna season varies in dates, not set by law, but rather by the tuna themselves. The first tuna usually start showing close to San Diego in late June or July, with the season peaking in August, and tapering off in September or October. Though in 2016 tuna were being caught offshore as early as April.

The Pacific Yellowfin tuna fishery is currently in an excellent state. Fishwatch sets a target range for fish populations, and Yellowfin have been above that target range for some time. In spite of the fact that they get absolutely slammed by sport fisherman, there is relatively little commercial market for the fish (compared to Bluefin and albacore), beyond mid-end seafood restaurants. Seafood Watch rates Pacific Yellowfin as a good choice for consumption.

There have historically been concerns of mercury poisoning from tuna. This is because mercury is absorbed by phytoplankton, which is eaten by sardines, which are in turn eaten by tuna. If each phytoplankton takes up just one nanogram of mercury (just my wild-ass-guess) then it really wouldn't be long at all before a tuna starts to have measureable levels of mercury trapped in its flesh.

That said, fisherman have favorably lower exposure to mercury than people who eat lots of tuna in a restaurant. Our tuna are in the 20-50 lb range, whereas the restaurant fish probably came from a 200-1000 lb monster. The larger the fish, the greater the bioaccumulation of mercury. Eating smaller fish minimizes your risk.

As I write this there are ongoing concerns of radioactivity in migratory species, especially those that swim near Japan and the Fukushima-Daiichi disaster. As a physicist and a fisherman, I have followed this story with great interest. I feel compelled to at least point out, that as of April 2016, no scientific evidence has been found of increased radioactivity in fish. Here is a particularly well-written article on the subject, for those interested.

As for food value, tuna is mostly meat. The gut cavity is relatively small and the ribs protrude only slightly into the side fillet. There is a central spine, with vertical spikes pointing up and down inside the fish. When the two fillets (one each side) are removed what's left is a spikey spine and head, like what a cartoon cat leaves behind after eating a fish.

Each fillet has a vein of dark meat running down the middle of its length. This is called bloodline. The tuna recirculates blood through this tissue to keep warm in cold water. Bloodline has a very strong flavor and generally is not consumed. The fillet is therefore cut lengthwise, above and below the bloodline so that it is removed. The top of the fillet is called the shoulder, and the bottom is called the loin. Although sometimes people refer to the shoulder as a loin as well. The skin is removed before consumption.

There are different preferences on the particular order of breaking down a tuna, but here is an excellent video showing my favorite way, as well as explaining some parts of the fish.

Once head, guts, bones, bloodline, and skin are removed the yield on a tuna is still quite high. At least 50% meat in nearly all cases, closer to 55% with a skillful hand, and up to 65% for large fish.

Yellowfin are commonly marketed as ahi, the Hawaiian term for red-fleshed tuna. The flesh varies from a dark pink in juvenile fish to a ruby red for mature fish. The texture is firm, the flake is thin, and the flavor is subtly fish-like, without being unpleasantly fishy.

Bluefin Tuna – aka Bluefin, BFT, ahi, toro (belly)

Bluefin tuna are cousins of Yellowfin and undoubtedly one of the most popular species of tuna, if not fish, in the world. Most of the facts listed above for Yellowfin are true for Bluefin, with a few exceptions.

One difference is that the Bluefin moving past California are, on average, larger than their Yellowfin cousins. On a day when everyone is catching 20 lb Yellowfin, a 40 lb Bluefin will come over the rail.

Another major difference is the state of the fishery. Whereas Yellowfin are healthy and abundant, Bluefin are overfished and in decline. Various scientists, governments, and regulatory agencies disagree about what the target population should be, but everyone agrees it is too low. At present it is listed at 4% of its recorded peak.

Bluefin tuna populations are extremely taxed by commercial fishing; mainly purse seiners. A purse seine is a giant cylindrical net. A spotting helicopter locates a school of fish, and the seiner moves in on one side of the school. A faster, smaller boat encircles the school with the net and closes it up at the seine boat. The net is then drawn up into a trap, with all the fish contained inside.

All over the Pacific, purse seiners capture entire schools of fish and haul them off to farms to be fattened up. If you are fishing in Mexico you will almost certainly pass the tuna pens. On a good (or perhaps, bad) day you will see multiple seine operations underway. If you do, the spotting helicopter will fly straight at your sport boat and hover there angrily like a guard bee.

There is a general consensus that Bluefin are better tasting than Yellowfin. With mature fish there is definitely a marked difference in both the color and fat content. Bluefin have a redder, sometimes almost purplish, flesh and are fattier overall. The belly of the Bluefin, the fattiest part of most fish, is particularly prized. The Bluefin will have thicker belly meat (pound for pound) than their Yellowfin cousins.

However in juvenile fish the difference is subtler. Sometimes there is very little color difference in the flesh of small fish. When served raw there is a noticeable difference. But as they are cooked, the two fish seem more and more alike to my palate. I think most people, in a blind taste test, would not be able to tell the difference in flavors of the cooked loins of juvenile fish.

As fishermen, what are our moral obligations when it comes to this fish? It is, without a doubt, overfished; yet in some years it can appear in misleading abundance off our coast. The presence of huge schools of Bluefin might lead us to believe their population is healthy, but we are looking at but a small, and not necessarily typical, sample of the whole Pacific.

Most sport anglers, captains, and deckhands, will keep a Bluefin without hesitation. They are likely to throw you over board if you even question that decision, let alone release one.

I must admit that I myself am torn. I certainly do not want to fish a species into extinction, especially a delicious and magnificent beast such as the Bluefin. However, I appreciate fishing as a way that normal people can obtain premium food ingredients that are otherwise expensive.

The day we declare Bluefin endangered and outlaw fishing for them, I will gladly and wholeheartedly stop targeting them and release any I do catch. However as long as purse seiners are scooping them up by the thousands for rich people, I think I can keep one or two. After all, it's the commercial guys wiping out species, not the homely fisherman with rod and reel.

As I write this, the limit for Bluefin anglers in California and Mexican waters is 2 fish. Little has been done to restrict the commercial catch; though they are also federally regulated, and the limits are revised every year. I am hopeful that conservation efforts will be applied across the board.

Bluefin tuna can look remarkably similar to Yellowfin. Both have a series of small triangle spikes running down their backs, which are yellow. Both can have yellow-ish tails. The keys to differentiating the two are the pectoral and second dorsal fins.

Firstly there is a primary dorsal on both fish, which is normally tucked down so that you hardly notice it. The second dorsal fin is non-retractable and sticks up above the center of the fish. It looks roughly like a triangle, or perhaps a shark-tooth shape. There is a matching fin, similar size and shape, under the fish's belly, mirroring the location on the top of the fish.

On a Yellowfin tuna these are always yellow. As the fish matures, they become extremely long and curvy, like a scimitar. A Bluefin will have the same first and second dorsal fin. On mature fish the second dorsal fins will be steely-gray to blue; hence Bluefin. However on juvenile fish these fins can be confusingly yellowish.

More telling is the difference in pectoral fins. When pressed flat against the fish's body, a Yellowfin's pectoral fins will reach back to, or beyond, the start of the second dorsal fin. On a Bluefin tuna the pectoral fin will typically not reach past the back of the first dorsal fin.

Sounds confusing, but look closely at the two images below. The top fish is a Bluefin tuna, the bottom is Yellowfin. Notice the top fish is generally bluer, but has slight yellow tint on the triangular fins running along the top and bottom of the tail. Look closely at the pectoral fin; it's much longer on the Yellowfin tuna. Here's another image and explanation from the web.

Bluefin tuna (top) vs Yellowfin tuna (bottom). Notice the elongated pectoral fin in the Yellowfin, as well as additional yellow coloration in the top and bottom fins.

Some people further identify one from the other by pointing out that the Yellowfin has a thick, yellow lateral line along its length, where a Bluefin does not. Once again, this method is less reliable with juvenile fish. The key, always, is the pectoral fins.

Both Bluefin and Yellowfin prefer warm water, usually low 70s. The Bluefin prefer slightly warmer water than Yellowfin. That might help explain why you find the big Bluefin mixed in with small Yellowfin; bigger fish can tolerate slightly cooler water than juvenile fish.

Albacore – aka longfin, albie, rarely - white tuna

Albacore is a strange variant of a tuna, with creamy white flesh and extremely long pectoral fins, reaching nearly to the tail. Their bodies are mostly silver, with a dark blue top.

Albacore has a milder flavor than the red-fleshed tunas. It has a bit more richness and a softer texture. Those two things typically mean people prefer albacore cooked to well or medium well (as opposed to seared, like ahi).

Its mild flavor lends itself well to being canned. Albacore tuna is among the most popular forms of canned tuna, but is generally considered the premium version. Albacore belly is a delicacy in Italy, where it is poached in oil and canned for later use on pasta.

Preferring cooler water, about 66 F, albacore typically only appear in years of cold water and bad weather. Otherwise they stay way offshore and don't hit the West Coast until they are near Seattle. That makes it difficult to sport fish them, since smaller boats don't like to venture far out to sea.

However, the commercial fisheries always bring home albacore in San Diego. In fact San Diego was once the tuna capital of the US. Chicken of the Sea was founded here and still maintains corporate offices. In the late 70s/early 80s the last of the San Diego canneries were closed due to dolphin-safe regulations. Commercial tuna fishing was moved out of the country and most of the US commercial fishing moved up the coast to Oregon and Washington.

The state of the albacore fishery is quite healthy. Like Yellowfin, albacore populations have remained consistently above target levels. It is rated as a good choice by both Fishwatch and Seafood Watch.

Note that though albacore is sometimes called white tuna, that (inexact) name is more commonly used for escolar, or butterfish. This is not a tuna, but rather a relative of the barracuda. Escolar cannot process some of the fatty acids they consume; consequently their flesh has an extremely high oil content. Consumption of escolar can lead to keriorrhea (from the Greek: flow of wax). I'll leave it to the reader to sort that one out.

Bigeye tuna

There are other tuna you might encounter offshore. The bigeye is nearly identical to the Yellowfin, with the exception of its big eye. Most people can't tell the difference. I really can't say much more about them, having never caught one or even seen one in real life. They are a rare catch in Southern California.

Bonito and Skipjack tuna

Bonito (top) and skipjack tuna (bottom) sandwich the tuna season. Both are edible, but considered inferior table far to the big 3 tuna species (Yellowfin, Bluefin, albacore).

Bonito and Skipjack are in the tuna family (*Scombridae*) but are of different genus. They are both much smaller than their color-finned cousins. Their flesh is oilier as well; with a much stronger, sometimes fishier flavor. Both are consumed worldwide nonetheless.

Skipjack are considered one of the world's most important fish. It is the fish most commonly found in a can of tuna. They live half as long as Yellowfin tuna and therefore breed twice as much.

21

Fishwatch considers their population above target levels, though they note the fish breed, and are caught, so quickly, it's hard to track a single group.

Skipjack and bonito are particularly important to sport fishermen. Tuna migrations depend on ocean currents and are therefore highly unpredictable. The arrival and departure dates of species, along with their length of stay, varies year to year.

However the fishermen's lore is: bonito precede tuna, and skipjack follow them. Supposedly when the landing counts start showing bonito, the tuna are near. And when anglers start catching skipjack, the tuna are nearly gone. That is scientifically unsubstantiated, but might be a useful guide for timing your fishing season.

Yellowtail – aka Yellowtail Amberjack, California Yellowtail, Hamachi, Yellows

Yellowtail, as it's called, is arguably the most important fish in Southern California. That's because it is the most reliably present fish off our coast. They are often found when tuna fishing, lurking under kelp paddies and floating debris. But they also reside around structure, such as deep-water islands and offshore banks.

Yellowtail can be caught locally, from to San Diego to Los Angeles, anytime the water is above about 64 F. Depending on those temperatures, they will hang at various depths. Yellows near the surface can be fished with either live bait or surface lures. Deep-water yellows are typically caught on yo-yo jigs, covered later.

On a really good year, the yellows can be present nearly year round. Several years ago huge yellows started showing at the Coronado Islands in early February. They disappeared briefly in the spring, but then made their reliable return for summer. Since about 2014, yellowtail have stuck around San Diego nearly year round; at least in small numbers. Even when the weather turns cold and rainy, the water offshore has remained in the mid-sixties.

Yellowtail range widely in size, especially with season. The fish can reach weights of up to about 100 lb. The spring yellows caught at the islands are often in the 30-60 lb range. Their size, along with their early/year-round availability, makes them an exciting catch. The summer yellows, hanging around kelp paddies, are typically much smaller; ranging from 5-20 lb.

Yellowtail are beautiful fish, long and sleek with a metallic green back and chrome belly. A stark yellow stripe separates the two and colors the tail. They sport the large eyes and forward-facing mouth of a serious predator. They are also some of the hardest fighting fish in the ocean and will invariably run to kelp if available. If you hook one near a paddy, put the brakes on and try to steer him clear of cover, lest he break the line.

The state of the yellowtail fishery is considered good. There is very little commercial fishing of the species; most Hamachi sold at sushi restaurants is farmed. The main human stressor of wild yellowtail is therefore sport fishermen. Seafood Watch considers line caught (which is how you'll be doing it) to be a Best Choice.

Yellowtail flesh is pearl white to pink, with small flecks that vary from pink to blood red. Like most ocean fish, yellows have a strong tasting bloodline that should be removed. Even the flecks of red and pink can sometimes have an intense fishy flavor. When cleaning yellowtail, I remove any hint of red flesh but leave the light pink.

Removing all the bloodline is a bit of a challenge. If you look at a cross section of the fillet, from the head-end, you will see what looks like two wings, or lobes to the fillet, with bloodline permeating up into the meat. If you simply skin the fish, most of the bloodline will remain with the meat.

Instead, the fillet should be cleaned from the flesh side. Lay a fillet on the cutting board, skin side down. There is an indented red line running the length of the fillet. Place the blade of your knife to one side of that indent and fillet out, away from center. Make a series of shallow, but long cuts. Imagine you are cutting a teardrop shape out of the fillet. This process will leave the central vein of bloodline with the skin.

Alternatively, you can simply cut about ¼ ince on either side of that red line. That will leave you with two, roughly triangular pieces of meat. Skin those triangles, flip them over, and shave all the bloodline away. Here is a good video demonstration. Here is a second (somewhat amateur) video of an expert chef turning a yellowtail into sushi; this one makes me proud to live on the west coast. (Notice, in particular, how meticulous he is about keeping everything clean – a key to great sushi).

The meat is extremely lean and will dry out if overcooked or frozen too long. But it is excellent raw, when cleaned properly. It is also exceptional on the grill with any good fish marinade, but I am partial to the Moroccan version I include later in the book. Yellowtail also smokes OK, but the lack of fat or flavor leaves the final product somewhat bland and generic. However I will take smoked fish over freezer burned fish any day.

Dorado – aka Mahi Mahi, Dolphinfish

I grew up calling this fish dolphin or mahi mahi, the former being the official American name for it and the latter coming from Hawaii. However the ones we encounter in San Diego are all immigrants from Mexico, where they're called dorado. Consequently dorado is what they're known as in SoCal.

Dorado are surface-dwelling, migratory species who follow warm water currents. They thrive in temperatures of about 83 F, but can be found in the much cooler waters of Southern California; typically high 60s. They can be found under kelp paddies, mixed in with yellowtail and tuna.

Without question, dorado are one of the most spectacular fish you can hook, at least in Southern California. They are striking, iridescent, metallic blue-green, with flashes of yellow. The males develop a large domed cranium, which makes you imagine they might butt heads to fight over their harems (which they certainly do not).

Dorado are also fantastic to catch because of their acrobatics. A hooked dorado will leap over and over again during the fight; changing color as they go. They are amazing creatures in the flesh but turn a dull (almost sad) grey almost instantly when they die. That makes most people feel guilty for killing them.

In spite of their color change, they are an insanely popular fish to catch for both commercial and sport anglers. Their meat is light, flakey, and has only a little bloodline to be removed; they make excellent table fare. The tropical looking fish inspires tropical flavors; I wish I was eating macadamia crusted mahi with mango salsa right now. With maybe a Mai Tai.

The dorado fishery is not tracked, but the population is considered strong. The fish grow quickly and begin spawning at 4-

5 months. They will spawn every 2-3 days and produce up to several million eggs per year. In spite of heavy sport and commercial pressure, they are considered a good choice by Seafood Watch. In Mexico they have the added protection of reduced catch rates: just 2 dorado count as a 5 fish limit.

Wahoo – aka Ono

Wahoo is an extremely long, grey and blue striped fish, with lots of sharp teeth. Naively, it looks like a huge barracuda, though it's not related. Wahoo are fast growing, migratory species. They start spawning at about 1 year and can live up to 10. They can reach sizes up to 200 lb.

Wahoo are sometimes solitary or will live in schools of 2-100 fish. They tend toward the warmest water, so they are actually a rare catch in San Diego. Most are taken deeper south in Mexico, and there are many around Hawaii. However, in 2014 a single wahoo was caught within close range of San Diego; the first on record. In 2015 multiple wahoo were caught in California waters;

my own step-brother landed three in one week, each weighing over 40 lb.

Wahoo populations haven't been assessed since 1999, but Fishwatch and Seafood Watch both consider it a good choice. Catch rates have remained steady, which is believed to indicate a healthy population.

Wahoo are excellent table fare, with large, firm-flaked white to greyish-white flesh. Like some of the other migratory white-fleshed fish, it has a good fish flavor without being overly powerful.

Opah – aka Moonfish

Opah are probably the rarest fish, you will most likely never see fishing in Southern California. The San Diego fleet will often hook under 10 in a whole season. Though in 2014, one boat caught 3 in one day.

Opah live in deeper water. They are mainly caught by commercial long liners while fishing for tuna, swordfish, etc. Some sport fishermen have mastered the art of fishing for them, soaking live baits for long periods; with perhaps some weight to carry the bait down.

The fish itself is also beautiful, ranking with the dorado as one of the most exciting things you can see at sea; perhaps more so because of its rarity. The body is like a big disk, round from the side but elongated-flat head on. It is red to purple-grey with white spots, and brilliant red fins.

The opah fishery is not well monitored because so few are caught. They are solitary animals, which makes it even harder to assess their numbers. Seafood Watch rates domestic (longline) opah as a good choice. And by all means, if you catch one you should keep it.

Opah is regarded as one of the tastiest fish available. It has four different kinds of meat on the one fish, ranging from light to dark. All are high in healthy oils, which give the meat a rich, creamy texture. The flavor is described as somewhere between swordfish and tuna.

Billfish – marlin, sailfish, and swordfish

Billfish are named for the long sword like protrusion from their nose. Swordfish are perhaps the most well-known of the group. They live and feed in deep water, only coming to the surface to warm up in the sun. It is rare (almost unheard of) for a sport angler to catch a swordfish, rather they are harpooned while sunning themselves.

Marlin and sailfish are both pelagic, surface species that can be caught in SoCal; with the main subspecies being the blue marlin. They used to be quite prevalent up around Los Angeles and around the Catalina and San Clemente Islands. However, heavy harvest of marlin, for decades, led to a decline in their numbers. But in recent years, with most fisherman practicing catch and release, marlin have begun to return to SoCal waters.

Still, marlin are a relatively rare sight. I once saw one busting bait on the surface, whilst I was at sea for work (not fishing). I had never seen one, really, in person until 2015, when (like other warm water species) a relatively large number of marlin were caught in San Diego.

Marlin grow up to 5' in their first year, and up to 11' over their lifespan of 10-15 years. At maturity they can weight up to 2000 lb. They travel solo, or in small groups, and can swim up 70 MPH.

When hooked, marlin will make repeated acrobatic leaps out of the water (sometimes endangering/injuring people in nearby boats). Imagine a 1-ton fish leaping out of the water; now imagine it leaping into your boat! I have heard that most sport boats don't bother trying to land marlin. Landing a 1000-2000 lb fish on 30 lb line is no easy feat, and many captains don't want to stop the whole trip so you can try.

Though they are a rare sight, both Fishwatch and Seafood Watch rate marlin populations as healthy and sustainable. This is helped greatly by the low catch/retention rates of marlin.

Though marlin are no doubt fun to catch, I have it on good authority that they, "taste good smoked." Normally, that is fisherman speak for it tastes like crap. Because they are so rarely seen, and would be a catch of a lifetime, and apparently taste like crap, I am a proponent of catch and release with these fish.

Chapter 2: Planning Your Trip

Anywhere there are fish worth catching, you can count on hiring a boat to take you to them. The charter boat system is a cornerstone of offshore angling. These boats rent space and sometime bunks, provide bait and food, and most importantly, will take you to the fish.

But when should you go? What should you fish for? Which boat should you take, and for how long? Those are the common questions that stump beginners. Let's break them down one-by-one.

The Trips

Trips are listed by length of time you will spend on the boat. Obviously the longer you are on the boat, the more time you will have to fish. More importantly, the longer the duration of your trip, the greater its range will be. Typically the pelagic, or migratory, species are further out, but in recent years they have come in as close as a few miles from shore. Here are the main types of trips available.

Half Day Boats

The shortest trips are called half day, and generally go from 6 am to noon, or noon (or 1) to sunset. These are short-range trips that will usually fish local kelp forests. A big fishing boat travels at 10 mph or less. Most boats are docked in a harbor or bay. Those harbors often institute 5 mph speed limits. That means the boat spends 1-1.5 hours just getting to the fishing spot and again returning home. On a 6-hour trip, easily half of it can be eaten up by transit time.

Half-day trips tend to stay close to shore. In San Diego, the kelp forests are right outside the bay. There you can catch local species such as calico bass, sand bass, and a variety of small fish that live in the kelp. Sometimes bigger fish like barracuda patrol the edges. And on occasion, yellowtail and white sea bass will hold up in the kelp, and you can have an exciting day.

In 2015 and the beginning of 2016, tuna came in as close as 3-4 miles from the shore in San Diego. Some landings have repurposed their half-day trips to chase these extremely local tuna. Since half-day trips cost around $50, this is an extreme bargain to get a shot at tuna. But be warned: these boats carry large numbers of anglers and often aren't set up to store large (and lots) of fish for extended periods. Spoilage is a real concern.

¾ Day Boats

These are trips that last most of the daylight hours. They depart at 6 am and return between 3 and 6 pm, depending on the quality of the fishing. This trip is long enough to allow 2-3 hours of transit time and still a good day of fishing.

In San Diego, the ¾ boats travel down to Mexican waters, around the Coronado Islands. There are resident rockfish on the pilings around the islands as well as halibut and kelp bass on the outskirts. For much of the year, resident yellowtail hang around the islands as well, at varying depths, and anglers will catch the occasional lingcod off the bottom.

During the recent years of exceptional fishing ¾ day boats have also had a shot at pelagic species such as tuna, dorado, and yellowtail.

Overnight Boats

Overnight boats are a 24 hour excursion. You will arrive at the docks around 8 pm and wait around, possibly enjoying a frosty beverage. Sometimes the boat will come in late from a previous trip, the deckhands will unload the fish, hose off the decks, and refill the galley with beer and food. A mob of haggard fishermen will file off the boat, looking exhausted but pleased. Tired, covered in blood and salt, and carrying away blue trash bags laden with fish; you will know they had a good day. Probably it means you will too.

The overnight boat will leave dock at 10 pm and motor out to the fishing grounds as you sleep. You will awake early in the morning: most likely you will be excited and will wake up when the motor revs down around 3 or 4 am. Otherwise you will be shaken from your bunk around 6 or 7 am by the enthusiastic screams of "HOOOK UPPP!" You'll then fish until about 2 pm, when the boat will make that heartbreaking turn homeward, and then you'll have a long waking boat ride home. The boat will pull in about 8 pm and the process repeats.

Generally an overnight boat is considered the minimum duration to catch tuna and pelagic species. Most tuna live in deeper water, and there's a lot of it out there. An overnight trip gives you lots of fishing time to find them. These deeper water fish will usually be much larger than those that the half and ¾ and ½ day boats can reach. These are the ones you want to catch.

I have been on trips of many lengths, and overnight boats remain my second favorite: a good compromise of time at sea, cost, and chances of success.

1.5 Day Boats

The 1.5 day, or day-and-a-half trips are my favorite variety. Like the overnight boat, you will arrive at the docks at night. You will board, motor all night, but then *fish all day*. On the 1.5 day boat you literally fish dark to dark: sunrise to sunset. Then you hit the rack, exhausted, as the boat motors home. You arrive at the docks rested, at 6 am on the third day, about 36 hours total.

Day and a half boats are a great time. You sleep on the boat twice. And while your first night is wrought with anxiety, the second night you sleep like a baby that's had 3 shots of tequila. You are covered with salt and (hopefully) fish blood, but the vinyl bed welcomes you like a mother's embrace.

Most importantly, on the 1.5 day boat you fish all day! That's great because most of the good fishing will be at sunrise and sunset. Those trips usually comprise a morning flurry of activity, followed by a 10-hour grind looking for kelp pads, and ending with a final, desperate, sunset surge to fill the boat. These trips will often cost 50% more than the overnight boats, but the chances of success go up by at least a factor of 2, in my opinion.

And did I mention you get to sleep on the way home? Don't underestimate how tired (and dirty) you'll be. Waiting in the galley or (worse) the sun, as you interminably crawl home is exhausting.

2 Day Boats

Two-day boats are starting to push the limits of long-range. A two-day boat is like an overnight plus a 1.5 day trip. The boat leaves at night, motors down to the grounds while you sleep, fishes all the second day, camps on the grounds the second night, and fishes until 2-3 pm the third day. In reality the third day is spent slowly motoring home, but nevertheless, 2 day boats are a much surer way to bring home some fish. The cost goes concomitantly up.

A warning though, two day boats are not for the faint of heart, or those prone to violent sea-sickness. We are talking about 48 hours on a boat; that's a long time to be uncomfortable if things go south. I suggest you try a number of overnight or 1.5 day trips first, to get your sea legs, before you venture into long range fishing.

Long Range Trips

This is where my first-hand expertise ends. There are trips, nearly year round, which range from 3-10 days, and probably more. These leave from San Diego, or Los Angeles, and head down deep into Mexican waters. Closer to the equator, the waters are warmer nearly year round and hold resident versions of all the fish described above and more.

These trips promise epic fishing, but be advised, there is an awful lot of steam time to get down there. Additionally, there are daily bag limits and possession limits for all fish. You are allowed to keep a certain number of fish per day, and you are allowed a certain maximum in your freezer or fish hold. The possession limit is usually equal to 2-3 days' worth of limits. So a ten-day trip is made of lots of travel time and lots of catch and release fishing.

The Landing

In places with any sense, multiple charter companies run their operations out of a common dock system. That creates a focal point of sport fisherman, boats, processors, and tackle shops. This area is often referred to as the landing.

To find the landing in your area you could Google "sport fishing (my city)". You could also go explore the port area until you see signs like "Point Loma Sportfishing", or "Fisherman's Landing".

The landing is the center of the action. There you can find out what boats are running, for how long, and what the catch is like. You could drive down to the landing and talk to people (UGH!). Or you could also cut to the chase and go right to the landing reports.

The Landing Count

The State of California requires all sport fishing boats to record their catch. Every day as the boats return, they call in their harvest to state commissioners. Whole websites are dedicated to publishing these landing counts, and the good ones collect detailed reports from successful captains.

The landing count isn't just there to taunt you. The experienced angler can glean reams of information just from one day's report. The inexperienced angler can learn to use it to break into the sport.

On its face, the report does appear to be a wanton celebration of fish death: 2,526 Bluefin tuna; 3,148 Yellowfin tuna; 5,823 yellowtail; etc. But by diving down into the numbers you can find out who is catching what, and where, and when.

The top level of a landing count lists a summary of all fish caught, so that's the first bit of information. The available and legal species vary over the year. Many of the big-game species are migratory. Their arrival and departure are dependent on ocean currents, and therefore, almost completely unpredictable. The landing report will tell you when those magnificent creatures have arrived in full force. By watching the counts, you can see when the season is ramping up, and when it starts to taper off.

In the 'off-season,' many of the sport boats chase local, smaller fish at the islands and kelp beds. Fish and Game code regulates the fishing of many of those species; but you don't have to memorize a rulebook! The landings know when (and where) they can fish for those species, and they will take you to the fish.

So check the landing report first to see what's in season and in abundance. On the West Coast there's always something.

Below the summary of total fish take, is a list of catches by charter companies. The charter companies are also themselves referred to as landings. In San Diego, the major 4 are Fisherman's, Point Loma Sportfishing, Seaforth, and H&M. These charter companies work as middlemen between boat owners and fishermen. They organize and book trips and reservations, collect fees, sell licenses, and usually have built in tackle, bait, and snack shops.

In short, you will book your fishing trip through a charter company. The landing report lists all such companies, and typically gives websites, addresses, and phone numbers for each. So that's the second piece of information: the landing count tells you what boats are running, where their operation is centered, and once again, what they are catching.

If you follow the links down to the landings, the catch is further broken down by boat and trip type. You can surf through the reports and judge if the tuna are in 2 day range, 1.5 day range, etc. As above, longer trips are much more expensive, and obviously, take more time. Fisherman really start to become ecstatic when boats in the 'overnight' and '1.5 day' range start getting into tuna.

In summary, use the landing count to see: what fish is in season and in abundance, where and what boats are catching them, and at what range. You see, the landing count is an invaluable resource for all offshore anglers, year round.

The best of these websites, and the one I check weekly, almost year round, is 976-tuna. They publish the saltwater landing counts, interviews and reports from captains, available trips, tackle deals, and even (somewhat sparser) freshwater details. The 976-tuna website is a critical resource to offshore angling.

Screenshot of 976-tuna from July 6th, 2016. A tough day for tuna fishing but yellowtails faithfully came to play.

The Season

There is always some form of ocean fishing on the West Coast. For much of the year, people fish kelp forests, rocks, and islands for rockfish and sand bass. On good days, these boats will encounter some of the big-game resident species like halibut and white sea bass. That can be exciting fishing: short trips, close to home, that provide an abundance of tasty fresh fish.

Around springtime, boats near islands start catching the first of the semi-migratory species: yellowtail. Unlike the tuna, which make a huge loop over the entire Pacific, the yellowtail tend to stay local. They have a water temperature preference, but tend to just

42

drift about in that comfort zone. Consequently sometimes yellowtail will start showing as early as February.

In those years it's easy to get excited for tuna season early. If the yellowtail are here in February, the tuna can't be far behind right? In reality that's not usually the case. In that year we had yellowtail in February, tuna fishing came late and was pretty sparse.

2014, was considered by many to be the best tuna season in at least recent history. The tuna and yellowtail started showing in large numbers about the same time, in May. That year was surpassed by 2015, where even though the fish didn't arrive early, they came in huge, and in large numbers. 2016, as of April, promises to be another banner year; El Nino always helps.

The main factor is weather. In Southern California we are blessed with good weather, on land and at sea. From spring through fall, the sea is mostly calm, winds are low, and the offshore swell is flat. That's because the prevailing currents and winds come down from the north. A series of off shore islands shield us from the really nasty stuff, and in the summer, allows warm water to seep up a bit from Mexico.

It's those warm water currents that bring the fish. But in winter the northerly patterns win out; bringing bad weather and bad fishing. Even in summer, strange weather patterns can break through. That can disrupt the migration; and boats will experience total skunkage for a few days, sandwiched between days of limit-style fishing.

But in general, you can count on offshore fishing for something, starting around February or March, and ending in November or December. As I mentioned, there is offshore fishing in SoCal for most of the year; and sometimes its entirety.

So seasons are unpredictable. Your results may vary. That's where the landing counts are your friend. Come May start checking them once a week or so. When you start seeing yellowtail, bonito, or even tuna, you know the season is ramping up.

That's when you have to make the first of many tough decisions: when to book your trip. Once tuna start coming in they will typically be here until September and sometimes into October. The season can be broken down into 3 main chunks: early, peak, and late.

The early season is marked by light crowds and spotty fishing. Boats might get limits two days in a row, get skunked on the third day, and be back on limits by the fourth. Early season is a gamble, but the pay-off is boats are typically running at half-capacity or less. It is such a luxury to be out on a nice big boat, and have it almost to yourself; even more so if you luck out with the fish.

By peak season word has got out that you are pretty much guaranteed to catch fish. Boats fill up early and are often booked over capacity. Some years you have to book weeks in advance (which is itself a gamble, since there are dips even in peak season).

Crowds are the pits on a tuna boat: other anglers stymie every move you make on deck, from the bathroom to the bait tank. The crowds make finding space to cast a bait, and fight a fish, difficult. A crowded boat just sucks; hence the derogatory moniker: cattle boat.

However fishing during peak season usually means you can get on the fish. I have been on many an early season trip where only a dozen, or fewer, fish are caught. It sucks to spend all that money and time to come home empty handed. After an early season failure, I usually find the crowds don't seem so unappealing.

Late season tuna fishing is honestly tough. As the season wears on, and the currents change, the tuna are further and further from the shore. I once fished a 2-day for albacore, in late September. The boat travelled 100 miles almost straight west into the open ocean. We were battered by huge waves, nasty wind, and spray the whole time. And like early season, we didn't even do that well. So I always try to hit it before or during the peak.

The Boat

There are many boats available for offshore fishing. Some are fixtures of the sport, and other come and go like, well, fish migrating across an ocean. Not all boats are created equal. Some are intended for offshore fishing and make every effort to create a successful and (somewhat) comfortable environment.

I have been on boats where there is scarcely enough deck space, and for that matter bunks, for half of the fishermen they are trying to carry. I have dodged many an asshole-deckhand; whose bitterness for working on a boat exceeded their enthusiasm to have a good time. There are all manner of unpleasant experience awaiting you at sea: good boats try to mitigate them and poor boats enhance them.

So before heading out and wasting your money, Google the boat you are considering. Chances are you can find some feedback about the vessel, as well as her crew and captain. Bear in mind that crews come and go, but captains are pretty steady. And a good captain starts with maintaining a good boat and a good crew. Bloody Decks and Yelp are both websites where I've found useful boat reviews in the past.

Perhaps most importantly though, you want to find a boat that will handle your catch well. Fish meat starts to degrade the instant blood stops flowing, even at refrigeration temperatures. A refrigerated fish hold is key to keeping your fish fresh. The best boats have a refrigerated saltwater (RSW) tank where they keep the fish. The saltwater has a lower freezing temperature, so your fish is kept as cold as possible, but still fresh. All good boats have this.

On the 'rally' years, like 2014 and 2015, short-range boats will try to glom onto the success of the tuna season. Boats that are built for ½ day trips, i.e. with no bunks or fish holds, will attempt ¾ day (or slightly longer) trips for tuna. They attempt to keep fish cool all day, in wet burlap sacks. Avoid these at all costs. You will be crowded and uncomfortable, and your fish will be rotten by the time you get home.

Chapter 3:   Gearing Up

I could write an entire book just on gear. It's tempting to do so, but it would be a surefire way to minimize readership. For now let's focus on the gear for the beginner. We will examine the basic properties of rods and reels, and then look at the typical combinations of the two. We will also cover terminal tackle, and the other stuff you need to bring along.

Rods

Everyone knows the main gear you need for fishing, is a fishin' pole right? Wrong. Poles are for flags and strippers; fishermen use rods. The rod is virtually always paired with a reel. Together, rod and reel are your weapons of siege in the deep blue sea.

The primary functions of the rod are two-fold: firstly it is a lever. You are going to be pulling against a large, strong animal; some mechanical advantage will come in handy. (*Give me a lever long enough, and a place to stand, and I shall move the world.*) The second purpose is to act as a spring. As you lift on that weight, or the fish surges out, the spring allows some instantaneous give in your gear, which prevents the line from snapping instantly, more on that below.

Rods are rated by several categories: length, weight, power, and action. When you look at a rod, it should have all these specifications written on its side, just above the handle.

Length

The first is obvious, the length of the rod. Longer rods tend to be springier, just by nature of their length. They give you a longer lever arm for casting: the longer the rod, the further the cast. Longer rods can sometimes make it harder to 'turn' the fish. Because they are springer, they don't have quite as much fortitude to moving a fish's head.

Weight

Weight does not refer to the mass of the rod, but rather, the weight rating of the line and the actual weight of the lure. All rods will have a line and lure weight listed on the side. For offshore fishing you will be dealing with a wide range of line strengths, but generally not much weaker than 15 or 20 lb, and not typically much stronger than 70 or 90 (at least in SoCal). Lure weights, even though the lure will mostly be a live sardine, range from ½ to about 3 oz.

Power

Power is a function of the rod's thickness at its base. The thicker the rod base, the stronger it is. For heavier fish, we will require a more powerful rod. In offshore fishing, you will need rods in the medium to heavy range.

Action

Action is the springiness of the middle and tip of the rod. You probably intuitively know that a strong spring will not stretch as much as a weak spring, given the same amount of force. Likewise, the strong spring will return to its rest position, faster than the weak spring, once that force is released.

Action is then a measure of how much the rod will flex, and how quickly it will return to straight: fast rods bend very little, slow rods bend a lot. In general it's easier to cast a fast rod. When we're hunting those tuna, we generally want a medium to fast rod.

Brands

There are many rod manufacturers; I would not attempt to list them all. Shimano, Cal Star, Seeker, Offshore Angler, and Ugly Stick are all popular brands, and among them, cover a wide spectrum of price and quality.

In San Diego, Seeker is widely regarded as the best rod, but you are likely to pay $150-350 for one. I am somewhat partial to Shimano; I like the quality of their gear and they have rods ranging from $15 to $300.

Reels

The purpose of the reel is also two-fold. First, the reel holds and organizes the line; there's an awful lot of it, so some organization is needed. Second, the reel applies friction, or drag, to the line spooling out. This is how you put resistance on the fish and also what keeps the line from snapping instantly; more on that below.

Reels also come in a variety of flavors. The two basic types are conventional and spinning. Conventional reels are also called bait casters, and sometimes come in a slimmed down version simply referred to as a casting reel.

Conventional Reels

Conventional reels got their name by virtue of being one of the first types of reels invented. In a conventional reel, there is a spool whose axis sits horizontal but perpendicular to the rod. The line winds directly on, or off, the spool: it is direct drive. The crank is usually geared so that 1 turn of the handle gives some larger number of spool turns. This is called gear ratio, and generally will be in the range of 4-7 for offshore conventional reels.

When you want to cast a conventional reel, you first disengage the gear and put the reel in free spool. This allows the spool to spin freely, which allows line to peel off; the only resistance is the angular momentum of the spool itself (and a tiny amount of friction – very small in good reels.) When you have made your cast, you either leave the reel disengaged, thus letting the bait/lure take more line, or you engage the reel and start cranking in. When you hook a fish, a slip bearing, or drag disk, presents some resistance to the line peeling off.

A good conventional reel has so little internal friction, that it can make casting challenging. When you throw the lure or bait, and line screams off the reel, you impart angular momentum in the spool. The reel is spinning at the exact speed as the lure's velocity through the air. When the lure hits the water it immediately stops its flight. If you do not thumb the spool at the exact instant the bait hits the water, the stored angular momentum in the reel will continue to spit line out. With nowhere to go, all that line starts to pile up around the reel, resulting in what's known as a rat's nest.

Casting Reels

Casting reels are a subset of conventional/bait casting reels. Often they are low-profile; with the reel body smooshed down around the line spindle. They are also engineered to help you cast lots of line off and reel it back in quickly and easily. They often employ magnet, or other 'dynamic friction' systems, that oppose the reel spinning without an active pull on the other end of the line. Casting reels are usually employed for much smaller species, like freshwater bass, but can be seen in larger forms out on the tuna boats.

Spinning Reels

Spinning reels are the sort that most anglers first learn to use. The axis of the line spool is parallel to the rod; which means the line has to change direction at the reel. On a spinning reel, the line comes down the rod to a half-loop of wire, called the bail. The bail re-directs the line motion from parallel to the rod to perpendicular to the rod. This sort of machine, which transforms one kind of energy or motion into another, is called a transducer.

The redirected line then runs to the bobbin. As you crank the handle, the bail spins around the bobbin, and the bobbin oscillates up and down. In this way, the line is piled nicely back onto the reel. When fish pull on the line, almost the opposite effect occurs. Except this time the bobbin spins with some resistance, again called drag.

Many anglers feel that the transducer makes this type of reel unsuitable for offshore use. Whenever energy is transformed, some is lost. The transducer is perfectly adequate for small fish, which make short runs. However under stress, these reels can sometimes fail due to their inherent inefficiency. By contrast, the direct drive and drag systems of conventional reels mean they can withstand long runs from large fish.

In spite of all that, reel manufacturers continue to engineer and sell spinning reels designed for offshore angling. They can overcome the inherent inefficiency of the design simply by beefing up all the parts, gears, drag disks, etc.

I must admit, for my own part, that I am often tempted to assemble and deploy a beefy spinning kit for offshore fishing. It would be fantastic in situations where I want to cast a lure or bait far from the boat. However, either from peer pressure, or a sense of tradition, I do not.

Brands

I have not used any of the offshore spinning reels, but the Shimano Baitrunner and the Penn Spinfisher are both popular choices. Either will cost you about $150. Cheaper options are the Shimano Socorro and Penn Fierce, both of which cost about $60.

For conventional reels, there are a number of good choices. The Penn 500 series are popular base models, for about $60-100. The Daiwa Sealine is a midrange option, for about $130. Shimano, once again, makes quality gear for a range of prices: the base model, Triton, will run about $140 and the top end, Trinidad, is nearly $500. There are high-end reels as well. Avet is the Corvette of offshore fishing but too expensive for my taste.

When you go offshore, you will see many different reels. But without exception, most will be a Penn 500s, Daiwa Sealine, or Shimano Torium. The Torium is my personal favorite, costing between $150-200 depending on size. It's like the Honda Accord of reels: reliable, insanely popular, and reasonably priced.

In fact, the Shimano Torium 20 is without question the best value in fishing reels and the most popular choice. However Shimano appears to have stopped making them for some time. As I write this, they are preparing to release a new version of it. Hopefully they haven't messed with perfection too much.

Rod & Reel Combos

Spinning rod and reel combos will be remarkably similar to those used by freshwater anglers, just much, much beefier. Be aware when setting up a rig, that spinning rods and casting rods are not the same. The transducer of the spinning reel sends the line coming off the reel into a much wider spiral. Therefore the line guides on a spinning reel are very large near the reel and become progressively smaller as they move up the rod.

So you can tell a spinning reel from a casting reel by the size of the line guides. If the bottom one is huge, it's a spinning reel. If they're all about the same size, it's casting reel. This is an important distinction, because even though you can mount either type of reel onto either type of rod, there is a wrong way to do it. Spinning rods are meant to bend forward, so to speak. The line is under the rod when you have a fish on. Casting rods bend backward, with the line above the rod.

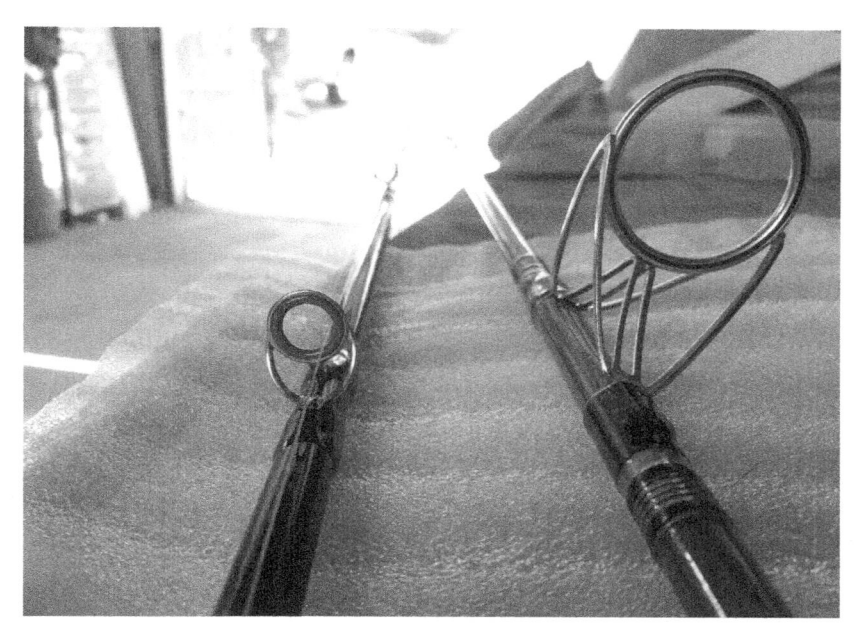

Casting rod (left) vs spinning rod (right) – notice the huge line guide for the spinner.

Because of this difference, the rods are meant to bend one way more than the other. If you hook it up backwards you are using the rod in the way it was not meant to bend, you are liable to break it. With all the time and expense of getting to the fish, and actually hooking one, the last thing you want is equipment failure in the middle of a fight. So make sure you are using the correct set up.

For casting rigs there are four basics purposes: 1) casting lures, 2) fishing live bait, 3) jigging or drifting the bottom, and 4) trolling. Each class of fishing requires a rod specific to the task.

Beginners should start out with a bait stick; fishing live bait is one of the easiest ways to fish. But in a pinch you can make short casts with it, and you can even jig the bottom with it. The bait stick is the all-around rig for offshore fishing, with jig sticks being advanced topics. I don't know anyone with a dedicated bottom rig (though I will speculate what it would look like) and trolling rigs are usually provided by the boat.

Bait Stick

Bait sticks are used to fish live bait, which are normally dropped right over the side or cast out a short distance. Choose a shorter rod, in the range of 6-7 feet, medium to heavy power, and medium action. These rods are used to muscle the fish; to turn his head.

A bait stick reel doesn't have to cast far, or retrieve fast. So it can be a beefy conventional, that once again, will turn a fish. A gear ratio of 4 or 5 is typical. Line weight should be somewhere between 20 and 50 lb, depending on the size of the fish you're chasing and the size of the baits you're fishing. A large sardine can pull 50 lb line, but a small anchovy struggles against 20. On banner years you may wish to have a big reel that can hold 80 lb line.

In practice you will not often know what bait you'll have or what fish you'll catch until you get out. I like to use 25 or 30 lb test as a good compromise between strength and weight.

Jig Stick

Jigs sticks are built for throwing lures, and therefore have a long nimble rod for casting and a reel with a fast retrieve. A jig stick should be a minimum of 8 feet, with medium power and fast action. You will want to throw lures in the range of 1-3 oz, with line weights of 25-50 lb.

These rods are usually sold as offshore jig rods. They typically do not have a reel seat, but rather a rubber wrapped butt. This allows the angler to choose the location of the reel, and therefore, the lever arm he has above and below the reel for casting. A typical choice for reel mounting is ~ 16-18" from the butt, which aides in casting and fighting the fish.

Pair the rod with a reel that has a fast retrieve; a gear ratio of 5, 6, or more. That will allow you to rip your lure through the water, or skip it along the surface. You might even consider a 'casting reel' with some of the fancier anti-backlash technology.

Bottom Rig

I don't do a lot of bottom fishing, so I don't have a dedicated rod for it. I use my bait stick. If I were going to build one I would consider the need to crank up heavy weights (> 4 oz) from great depths. I would choose a medium length rod, about 5-6 feet, with heavy power and slow action.

For reels I would look for something with a lower gear ratio, about 2 or 3. Like riding your bike up hill, you will want to make more/easier turns. Heavy line is also called for, in the 30-60 lb range.

Trolling Rig

Trolling rods are short, less than 6 feet. The reels are large and hold lots of line, with a moderate gear ratio of 4 or 5. Extremely heavy line is used, often up to 80-100 lb test, to withstand the fish being pulled by the moving boat. All boats are equipped with trolling rigs, but for some reason, on every trip, there's a guy who brings his own.

Rod and Reel Combos

	Rod				Bait Caster Reel	
Type	Length	Weight	Power	Action	Line Strength	Gear Ratio
Bait Stick	6-7 ft	25-50lb	Med-Heav	Medium	25-30 lb	4-7:1
Jig Stick	8 ft +	25-50 lb	Medium	Fast	30-40 lb	5-7:1
Bottom Rig	5-6 ft	30-60 lb	Heavy	Slow	50 lb +	2-3:1
Trolling Rig	5-6 ft	80-100 lb	Heavy	Medium	80 lb +	4-5:1

To Buy or Lease

The time and expense of going offshore mean you can't afford equipment failures. If you bring your rod offshore, be sure it's in good working order before you leave. I have lost fish due to old line, old reels, and I've witnessed broken rods.

For these reasons, check your gear before you go out. Change the line to see if it seems old or worn. Rinse your gear when you're finished, and store it out of the sun. I also recommend you don't go to sea with only one rig. It's easy to get carried away with gear, but I usually like to bring a light, medium, and heavy rig.

My heavy rig is lined with 40 or 50 lb test and could also serve as a good bottom rig. My medium rig is my go-to: a Torium 20 on a Shimano Talevera medium heavy 6'6" casting rod. It's spooled with 30 lb test and I can use it to fish bait or cast a lure. For a light rod I have a smaller casting reel on a medium light rod, with 20 lb test. I can cast far with it or fish a small bait like an anchovy.

From all this you can see that offshore fishing requires some expensive gear. You get on that boat with five or six hundred dollars' worth of rods and reels. Many anglers build up their arsenal over time. However a legitimate option is to rent.

The landings all rent bait sticks and sometimes jig sticks. Cheaper versions sport the Penn 500 reels, but some shops also rent a nicer set-up with a Torium. These rentals are on the order of $20-30 per day. Which is actually a screaming deal considering it can cost upwards of $200-300 to set up a rod and reel combo. I know many people who rent a rod, or even a spare for a trip, and it's an economical option.

Consider also that a rental rod can be tailored at the moment of rental, to the trip you are taking and the fish you are targeting. The landing is routinely swapping out line on their rigs to match the fish the boats are finding. And the landing crew meticulously checks and maintains all gear, to ensure quality rentals for their customers. There is definitely a strong argument for renting gear, especially when you are just starting out.

Line Choice and Drag

This is probably one of the most important concepts of fishing, which is why I've buried it in the middle of the book. People often believe that you need big line to catch big fish. The problem is, big line is hard to fish and often spooks the fish; especially the bigger, older ones you're after.

People are often surprised that I am fishing tuna with 25 or 30 lb test. "I hope you don't hook up a big Bluefin today...," they chortle. Let me lay down some basic concepts here:

1. *A fish does not pull his weight.* That is, a 20 lb fish does not pull on your line with 20 lb of force. It's a much more complicated arrangement, what with the fish actually kind of weightless but propelling itself through the water. The pull *is* a function of the size of the fish, *but also* the kind of fish, and its particular spirit to fight. Sometimes you reel a huge fish right up to the boat and net him before he even knows what's happening. In fact, it's smaller fish that often have the most fight per pound.
2. *The spring of the rod protects your line from shock.* It's a scientific fact that for a given system, static friction is greater than kinetic friction. Put another way, it's harder to get something moving than to keep it moving. When a fish surges, the line/reel system must overcome that stationary friction before it can enter the steady-state moving friction regime. That means there is an instantaneous shock to the system which could break the line, except the spring of the rod absorbs it.
3. *There is more drag than you think.* All reels have a maximum amount of drag. You can dial it in by turning the drag wheel or disk and even measure it with a spring scale. But the fish also has to pull all that line

through the water. Believe it or not, pulling a couple hundred yards of monofilament through the water is not effortless. Furthermore, the more line he pulls of the reel, the lower the torque radius on the spool. He has to overcome a greater moment of inertia in the reel and thus has effectively more drag there. He also has to make that initial surge to get the drag moving and rod bending, which tires him. When a fish runs for more than 3 or 4 seconds it starts to seem like he will run forever. But the further he runs the more drag he creates for himself, and the faster he will tire.

Through clever use of drag it is possible to catch very large fish with very light tackle. The Torium 20, can only exert 20 lb of drag on a fish. If you are using a springy rod, and 25 lb test, and perfect line/knots, it's impossible for a fish to break that line without running it all off the spool. A properly designed, and well maintained, system typically will not fail you.

In those extreme cases, where someone has a properly designed system but hooks a whale, the boat must simply chase the fish until he tires. This is impractical in open-party boats, but you can see it really destroys the big-fish/light-line barrier. I have watched Tred Barta (on TV) land 100 lb+ sail fish on 2 lb test.

All that said, there are practical limits. And there is an opportunity cost to fighting a fish too long. I have been on trips with guys who fish teeny-tiny reels, with maybe 10-15 lb test. They laugh at everyone else's rods, spooled with 'rope.' But I've seen those same guys struggling for 1 hour, with a fish I could land in 15 minutes with 30 lb test. So while they're 'sporting it out' with one fish, for an hour, I've already landed 3 or 4.

And even the most skilled angler can make a mistake, or get screwed by other factors, the longer the fight goes on. Last year I hooked a monster Bluefin on 30 lb test. I fought him for 40 minutes, during which time he made so many deep runs my back and arms were burning in pain. During that long fight, I got tangled with other anglers fishing abrasive line, three times. On the third time, my scuffed up line finally gave out. At that point I grabbed my 50 lb rig and cast back out there.

You don't get to go tuna fishing that often. And when you do, you're not getting bit all the time. You should always strive for the compromise of the heaviest line your bait can handle, that will still get bit. Most days my opening salvo is 30 lb.

Terminal Tackle

Hooks

One of the great joys of offshore angling is its simplicity. I do bring 3 rods aboard, but typically no tackle at all. I have the line on my reels and a small box of hooks in my pocket.

Below I will cover the methods of fishing, but the most common is with live bait. You simply hook a live sardine or anchovy on and let him swim. Hook sizes are always 1/0, 2/0, or 3/0 in SoCal, so I actually bring all 3. But 2/0 is most common so that's what's in the box in my pocket.

Line

For line, as I mentioned, 30 lb is my go to choice, and my heavier rig is currently lined with 50 lb test. The line on the reel is actually divided into three parts. Right up against the reel, the first few hundred yards of line is called the backing. The next 100 yards of line is called a top-shot, and the final 2-3 yards of line is the leader. Now in practice, you could spool the whole reel with 30 (or 50) lb monofilament and be done with it. Then all three parts are the same.

However, many people, including I, choose to use different lines for each section. For backing I like to use braided line. It is more expensive than mono, but much lighter for a given strength. I currently have about 300 yards of 50lb PowerPro braided line on both my medium and my heavy rig. That allows me to extend my reach of line, by probably 40-50% for the medium rig, and 20-30% for the heavy rig.

My top shot is plain monofilament, in 30 or 50 lb test. And for leaders I always use fluorocarbon monofilament. Fluorocarbon has different index of refraction from regular nylon mono line, and it is supposed to be invisible to fish. If you compare fluorocarbon and traditional mono line underwater, you will find that it is decidedly not invisible. It does seem harder to see, but that could just be the hype talking. Fluorocarbon is more expensive, but you only use 6-10' at a time, so a little bit lasts awhile.

A side note: in fresh water I always fish straight 10lb braided line, with just a 6' leader of 10 lb fluorocarbon. The 10 lb braid is much lighter than monofilament, and I can really cast the shit out of a ½ oz lure with that set-up. Braid also has significantly less stretch than mono. So you can run it tighter and get a better feel when working a lure along the bottom. You also get a better hook set, when you have a lot of line out.

I once tried the same experiment on my medium tuna rig. I spooled hundreds of yards of 50 lb braid onto the reel, and finished it with a 6' fluorocarbon leader. The benefits of this system were clear to me:

- I could fish any leader from 20-50 lb, and the sardine wouldn't really know the difference (since braid is so light), while having the backing of 50 lb strength.
- I would have a better feel on the bait when I had 100-200 yards of line out, by virtue of having zero line stretch.
- I could use the braid's abrasive nature to saw through kelp if I ever got tangled up.

The experiment was short lived. It is the abrasive nature that makes braided line somewhat rude on boat with large numbers of people. Upon boarding a boat I was immediately notified by the captain that my ingenuity was NOT appreciated. Braided line, he informed me, had a greater tendency to bunch up in the water, especially around the boat, which would cause more tangles. Once tangled, that braided line would cut through everyone else's mono.

That trip I did my best to stay away from other anglers, many of whom called me stupid and a dupe for buying the expensive line. I also was very careful to never let my line pile up in coils on the surface, as it was supposedly prone to do. I managed to avoid nearly all tangles, didn't cost anyone a fish, and immediately reverted to a mono top shot when I got home.

It's also worth noting, that on my last trip, we had about a half dozen noobs, who were fishing straight braid. Sure enough, their line piled up, encircling mine. And when my line went guitar string tight to that fish of a lifetime, I had all kinds of braided lines wrapped around mine. I had to stop fighting the fish so the deckhands could unravel the mess, not once, not twice, but three times. And on that third time I felt the telltale 'plink' that lets you know your fish has come off the line.

All I can say is: don't be that guy. Be a good citizen on party boats and fish mono, at least on your top shot.

Sinkers/weights

Some people use weights, I never have. The pelagic species are hunting the surface zone of the water column. The live bait will sometimes skim the surface and sometimes dive down. Some people even claim if you hook the bait in the nose he swims up and if you hook him in the butt he swims down. I can't corroborate that theory.

In either case, some people like to weigh their baits down. The theory is: big fish, like Bluefin or opah, hang a bit deeper. It sounds nice, but I have seen a lot of people using weights, and I have never seen an opah hooked or landed. Nor have I ever seen one of the weight-guys catching big Bluefin when no one else is. So I don't bother with weights.

Lures

Lures can be fun but require skill to cast them. I will cover lure techniques below, some that even do not require casting, but for now here are the basic types.

Swimbaits

These are like little rubber fish, with paddle tails. You pin them onto a hook with a weighted head (called a lead-head or jig). The lead-head and paddle-tailed rubber fish make a nice little lure that can cast far, sink as deep as you like, and make a nice swimming action on the retrieve. The lead-heads cost $2-3 each and are reusable. The rubber fish is often destroyed after catching one or two fish, but these are deadly lures that don't cost much.

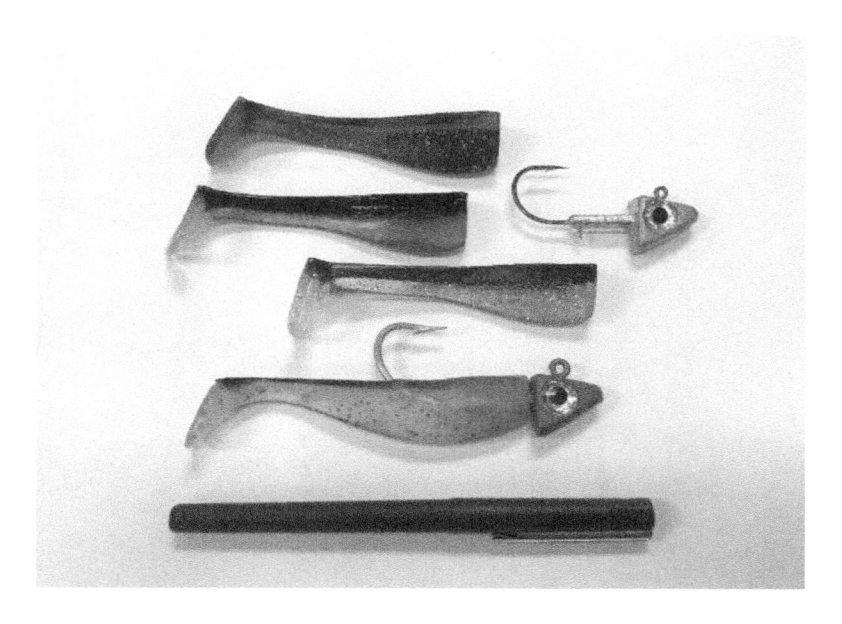

Spoons and metal jigs

Some of these are called spoons, because they are concave pieces of shiny metal with hooks. Metal jigs are usually rather fish-shaped. Most are shiny, colorful, and heavy - therefore fun to cast. One of the more popular versions in the last few years is the brand Megabait, but there are many varieties of this style. The best patterns are silver, blue, green, and black, to emulate the native sardines and anchovies of the Pacific. These can be more expensive, ranging from $5-20, depending on brand.

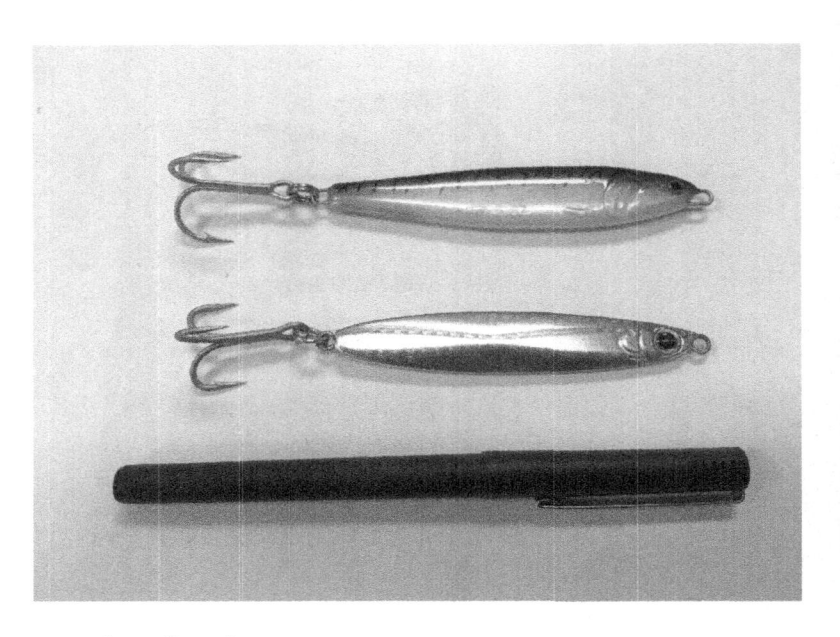

Yo-yos and surface irons

This is a particular brand and style of lures. They are molded metal (for bottom fishing), or ceramic (for skimming the surface), shaped like a long flattened football. Both are particularly effective for Yellowtail, sometimes on top (surface irons) and sometimes at the seafloor (yo-yos). Strangely the most popular pattern is 'scrambled egg' – white and yellow. Both cost about $5-10.

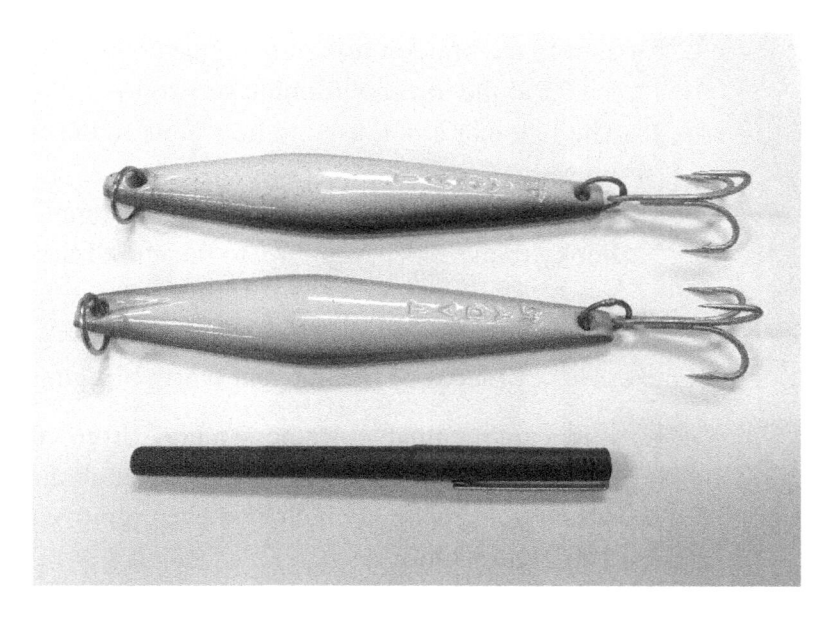

Crankbaits and surface plugs

Tuna are voracious predators, like bass but perhaps more so. Rapala and other crank bait makers produce large hard baits for offshore fishing, even surface poppers. Imagine catching a tuna on top water! Your life will never be the same. These vary widely in price, according to brand, but expect to pay at least $10-20.

Knots

In the history of human ingenuity, knots have received more than their fair share of attention. I own several books on knots, including *The Encyclopedia of Knots and Fancy Rope Work* (yes, that's a real thing); a nearly 700 hundred page book with half a dozen to a dozen knots per page.

Relax though, I typically only use two knots when tuna fishing. On a rare day, I might use three. Those three knots, and how to tie them, are:

1. The Double (or Triple) Surgeon's Knot. This is used for line-to-line connections; mating your monofilament top

shot to the braided backing (triple surgeon), or your leader to the top shot (double surgeon.)
2. The Palomar Knot: used to tie a hook to the end of the line.
3. The San Diego Knot; used to tie more complicated and hooky things, such as a lure, to the end of the line

Other Gear

Some other key pieces of fishing gear worth bringing along:

- Pliers are invaluable. Remove a hook from your fish, cut your line, remove a hook from your clothes, turn a nut on your reel in a pinch, and even remove a hook from your hand.
- Nippers are a great, cheap and lightweight addition. I bought mine at a fly fishing shop and they hang around my neck with my fishing license. They are superior at cutting line to my pliers and always handy.
- Fighting belts are nice if you're a scrawny little puke like me. They can be purchased at some sporting goods stores, or at the landing, for about $15. When you fight a fish you will jam that rod butt into your gut until you want to barf. Some morons say not to put them on until you're fighting a fish, which defeats the purpose entirely. And some tough guys don't use them at all, which confounds me.
- Knuckle tape is basically medical tape with superior waterproofing. It looks silly when you see anglers wrapping their knuckles like boxers. But after your first day of fishing you forefinger will be all line cut and you'll be wishing you had some.

Clothing, sun protection, and footwear

The offshore fishing weather in SoCal is beautiful. The peak of the season is in August; San Diego and LA are boiling over in the 90s and low 100s. At sea the temperatures are a pleasant 70. Low swell, light winds, and on a good boat, very little spray.

Be prepared though. Nights are cool, and rough weather and surf can leave you soaked. This can be addressed in one of two ways: 1) wear quick dry clothing, or 2) don't get wet.

Many anglers opt for shorts, T-shirts, and flip-flops. They weather the storm like men and stand there dripping cold and wet in the wind. I always opt for weatherproofing. I bring lightweight waterproof pants and a jacket that slips over my clothes. I wear cheap rubber 'wellie' boots to keep my feet dry. (Sometimes the deckhands hose down the whole boat, and you, while you're standing there.)

Seriously, bring a hat and wear sunscreen. Even in pleasant weather, I wear lightweight long sleeves, pants, and even an UPF facemask. The sun is intense out there coming down from the sky and bouncing up off the water. It comes at you from all directions, and sometimes there is precious little shelter.

You won't believe the number of sunburns you will see on a tuna boat. Many recreational anglers are largely pencil pushers and office workers. In the morning you will see a bunch of pasty white dudes, and by the end of the day there's a ship full of bloated lobsters. It's like they've never heard of the sun before. Protect yourself.

Chapter 4: Get Onboard

You've scouted the season, you've booked your ticket, and maybe assembled some gear. Now it's time to head down to the landing. Here a few tips that will make your trip more comfortable.

Packing and Parking

Most landings, inexplicably, have woefully little parking. I guess waterfront property is expensive. This sucks when you're fishing, because you are probably carrying a bag, a few rods, and a tackle box with you. And when you return you will probably have a ton of fish. There is no easy answer other than to go with a buddy. One of you can guard the stuff while the other shuttles the car around. There are usually a few unsavory types wandering around the waterfront too; so seriously, don't leave expensive gear unattended.

Get to the landing at least an hour before the trip leaves. You are likely to be sitting around the docks for a while, but you'd just be sitting at home anyway. And if you don't like sitting around, maybe fishing isn't for you. Most of the time you will find a purveyor of sudsy refreshment and probably fish tacos near the boats, and it gives you an opportunity to see what people are catching. Some keen enthusiast's even fish from the docks. They normally don't let you do that, but if you're standing there, waiting to get on a boat, with all your gear, who's going to stop you.

Find your bunk

The first thing you do when you get on the boat is put your gear down. If it's an overnight or longer trip, you will be sleeping on the boat, so you'll have to choose a bunk. The most common choice is to grab a bunk high up, on the sides of the boat. This is the wrong choice.

The main motion you will feel on a boat is side-to-side rocking. That's partly due to the geometry of the boat. Roughly speaking the average aspect ratio (length/width) of a boat is about 3. That means a boat that is 50 ft long will be about 15 ft wide.

Now imagine that boat hits a swell that is 6-7 feet. If the boat hits the swell head-on, you have a wave that is about 10% of the relevant length scale (the length of the boat). If the same wave hits the side of the boat, now it is about 50% of the relevant length scale (the width of the boat). Which one do you think will be more noticeable?

Let's look at the exact math. Take a 50 ft long boat that is 15 ft wide. Assume we have a 6 ft wave that is A) under the bow of the boat or B) under one side of the boat. In case A we have arctan(6/50) ~ 7°. In case B we have arctan(6/15) ~ 22°. In short, the disturbance is three times as great for a crossing wave, so that's the motion you will feel more.

The second reason is due to the way a boat fishes. When you find fish the captain kills the prop and the boat glides for a bit before it stops moving. At that point it is drifting with the wind and tide. An object drifting in the wind tends to orient with maximum surface area with respect to that wind. In other words, after a time the boat will be at 90° to the wind.

The wind is the major source of waves out there. Since the wind is pushing the water, the wave crests are also oriented 90° with respect to the wind direction. Therefore as you are drifting in the wind, wave crests are hitting the boat on the side. And we already know what happens when waves hit the side (see above).

Why are we doing all this math and stuff? We have proven that a boat mainly rocks side to side. An object rocking side to side will have an axis of rotation running through it, roughly along the center of its long axis. Physics will tell us that the least amount of movement occurs at the axis of rotation. Think about a seesaw...a person sitting over the teeter-point will experience less motion than the people sitting on the ends.

From all this it's hopefully clear that the bunks with the least amount of movement are those that are closest to the axis of rotation for the side to side rocking. The cross-wise center of gravity for a boat will depend on its height and its keel. But almost without exception that axis will lie near the bottom of the bunkroom, and certainly centered lengthwise.

Therefore the correct bunk, assuming you want to minimize rocking motion (and take it from me, you do), is in the bottom center of the bunkroom, not the topside. Fortunately for you, most people are morons and don't know basic physics and math. Furthermore they probably won't read this book. The upshot is that even if you are late getting to the boat and choosing your bunk, the good ones will likely still be available.

Signing in

Once on the boat, gear down, and bunk chosen, you will have to sign in. This is where they deckhands will register your arrival on the boat. At that time they will give you a number. Often they will give you a slip of paper with that number printed on it. *This exercise isn't just for fun, the number has meaning and will affect your experience on the boat and afterward!*

The primary purpose of your number is to keep track of your fish. When the flurry of activity hits, fish will hopefully be coming over rail at an extremely fast pace. When you rush back to the fish hold with your catch they are going to ask you, "What's your number?" That's so they can label the fish by the person who caught it. They do so by stapling a piece of paper with your number to the gill plate.

If you don't know your number at that time, and/or have to fumble around looking for your slip you are screwing up the system! In the very best case you are slowing the deckhands down, clogging up the valuable real estate near the fish hold, and just generally annoying. In the worst case your fish might be accidentally assigned to someone else. Once that fish goes in the box with a number, it's impossible to change ownership, so get it right.

The second purpose of the number is to determine troll order. We will cover trolling below, but for now know that you will be required to stand post over a line that is being towed behind the boat.

So firstly you must know your number so you know when you are being called to duty. Manning the troll lines is an essential job on the boat, and I have never seen a boat where it works perfectly. Please know your number and listen for when you are called up.

There are typically 4 trollers at any given time on a boat. Sometimes you will be required to troll for hours. If you are fishing with friends, it will be nicer to troll with them. So try to get a number adjacent to your friends and hopefully contained with a 4-group (i.e. 1-4, 5-8, 9-12, etc). That's especially good when you need to ask someone to watch your line for a sec, while you hit the head or grab a drink (which you should try to avoid doing, while trolling – but sometimes nature calls).

Lastly be aware that trollers are called up in order. Trollers 1-4 will be the dawn patrol, the first ones manning the troll in the morning. It is hard to get up first thing when the captain comes on the radio to wake everyone up. But those first four trollers are pole position. Morning bites are famously good and trollers 1-4 are primed to catch something first. Having a low number is a trade-off: shitty sleep but great fishing.

Your number also has bearing on how your fish is handled. At the end of the trip, on the way home, all the fish will be stacked on deck so you can take photos and the deckhands can fillet the fish.

They start cleaning fish for angler no. 1 and finish by cleaning the fish of the last guy (angler no. 36). If you are number 36, your fish sits out of the RSW for a long time waiting to be cleaned.

If it's night time, it's not too big a deal. But during a sunny day the deckhands have to hose all those fish down every few minutes to keep them cool. I can't imagine that improves the quality of the meat, but I will never know. Check in as quickly as possible. I always try to keep my number in the low double digits and my fish out of the RSW for minimal time.

The final, and perhaps most important, reason for your number is to pick up your fish afterward. When the boat docks you will get your gear, de-board the boat, and walk the 100 yards to the dock. In the meantime the deckhands will unload the fish from the hold, pack it in a cart, and wheel it up to the docks.

In that short journey the deckhands will most likely forget they ever met you. They won't know your name, and they won't recognize your face. Some people get offended by this, but try to be sympathetic to the fact that they see a non-stop parade of anglers all summer. Surely the names and faces run together.

At the dock the deckhand will start picking up bags and calling out numbers. When he calls your number, assuming you have managed to remember it, then you can claim your fish. In the likely event he doesn't recognize you, he will ask for your receipt. On my last trip offshore an old dude got pissed, because no one had told him to save his number stub. Don't be that guy.

Food and drink

The next thing to consider on the boat, once you have a bunk and a number and are waiting to actually reel in a fish, is what to eat and drink. Let me be the first to break the unfortunate news to you. Food on a boat is OK at best. You won't want to eat it all, because you'll be feeling crappy from little sleep and mild seasickness. And its crazy expensive.

They typically have a system where sodas, water, and chips are $1. Beers are $3, and for all-day coffee it's $5. You mark a tally on a sheet for each one you take; honor system. The actual meals are nebulous and their prices are shrouded in mystery.

Breakfast is usually a burrito: eggs, potatoes, bacon, cheese, and salsa. Some people get this combination without a tortilla. Some people eat it on bread. Apparently you can negotiate with the cook, and he decides what to charge you according to his whim.

Lunch is usually sandwiches, or burgers. Once again, a variety of choices result in a mysterious pricing scheme. Dinner will often be seared tuna (or in poor fishing years, chicken), sometimes stir fry, and very rarely, a cheap steak. Often dinner includes some form of salad and dessert.

I seriously cannot stress enough that the system for getting what you want, and how much you will pay, is completely opaque. My last trip I had coffee, two beers, a burrito, and the fish dinner. I was charged $45.

Some trips come 'all included' which means the meal cost (but not drinks – not even water) is included. If you think that's a good deal, then I also have a piece of the London Bridge I'd like to sell you.

All this is not meant to be a complaint, necessarily; although the system is primed for abuse. I think you could easily offend a cook and suddenly he feels your burrito was definitely the $10 kind, and not the run of the mill $6 sort. No, this isn't a complaint but fair warning. I like the burrito for breakfast and coffee is essential. But I can easily pack a PB&J, some granola bars and apples, and 2L of water and save myself $20-30.

A word of important warning: under no circumstances should you bring a banana on the boat, unless you are said boat's owner. There is a powerful superstition among fisherman that fish hate bananas. It is complete garbage of course, unfounded by science. But people can be quite passionate about these things, and you are bound to come across some hard characters on these boats, with whom you DO NOT want to have a frank exchange of views – especially over bananas.

And another thing, the beer is almost always shit. Which is pretty inexcusable in SoCal.

Seasickness

People often say, "I'd love to go deep sea fishing, but I get seasick." I want to take this opportunity to clue you into a few secrets.

1. I almost always get, at least a little, seasick.
2. Anyone could get seasick in the right circumstances.
3. Even the deckhands get seasick! (On my last trip, one of the deckhands had a patch behind his ear)

There are many misconceptions about seasickness, but it's an albatross all sailors must carry round their neck. Many people believe that if they never get seasick, then they never will. Not true, I went offshore with a Russian who had spent 6 months on a research vessel. Before we had even left the bay, in a 50 ft boat, he was flopped down like a walrus on the bow of the boat.

Conversely some people believe "you get used to it." I put that theory to a Navy sailor I once met. He spent 4 years, off and on, a massive aircraft carrier in the Pacific. His exact words were, "I was sick the whole time."

In truth I believe seasickness is a matter of degrees; it depends on a lot of variables. It's something you can manage, to a point, if you keep your wits about you. Furthermore you are inevitably going to feel shitty on boat at some point. Whether from sleep deprivation, greasy food, exhaust fumes, heat exhaustion, or good old fashioned green-gills, there will be at least a brief time where you will not feel as snuggly comfortable as you do in your own home.

People are often adverse to taking motion sickness drugs; almost as a point of pride. If you are going to spend hundreds of dollars on a fishing trip why risk it? Dramamine is the most famous of the over the counter drugs. I find it makes me drowsy, and I feel woozy for days even after getting off the boat. Furthermore you have to swallow it. There will be times when keeping something down is a challenge; that's not the time you want to get into a vicious logic circle. (I feel like puking so I need Dramamine. I can't take Dramamine because I'll puke it up…)

Bonine is the less well known, but better option. It is chewable and the taste is not completely disgusting. You only need it once every 24 hours. It's available OTC. It doesn't make you drowsy at all. And best of all, it really sort of works.

The hardcore guys use Scopolamine patches. They are only available with prescription, and I can never remember to ask my doctor when I'm there. Consequently I have never tried them, but I'm told they work quite well. It is common to see people donning half a patch behind the ear. (Off-label studies also suggest that Scopolamine helps with chronic depression – but you're a fisherman, so that's not something you need to worry about.)

All that said, there are a number of tricks I use to stave off seasickness:

- **Take your medicine**. Take one 12-24 hours before the trip. Having it 'in your system' seems to give you a head start on the seasickness. Really there is no risk in taking it, and it's insurance against a terrible trip.

- **Get a good night's sleep**. Which, by the way, is virtually impossible on a boat. The boat is rocking all night. The bunk itself is hard and made of vinyl. The bunkroom is bright, and full of engine noise and diesel fumes. Wear a sleep mask and earplugs, and choose the right bunk.
- **Keep your stomach full**. It's counterintuitive, but having a full stomach helps fight seasickness. Sometimes you really have to force that food down, and you feel like it's the wrong choice. But trust me, your stomach will be happier trying to digest something than having its juices sloshing all around. I always bring a few apples and some peanut butter sandwiches.
- **Stay hydrated.** Your body does not function well when dehydrated. And you will be especially prone to it when standing out in the wind and sun all day. Drink lots of water. Bring some from home in fact, because they charge you for this life-sustaining substance on the boats. Some people believe if they stay drunk the whole trip they will a) have more fun, and b) be less prone to seasickness. I have not found either to be true.
- **Get some air.** When all else fails, find the windiest place and put your face in it. This gives you a two-fold effect in that you have lots of oxygen to breathe, and you will typically be facing the horizon. People often start to feel sick when they go to the bathroom or the galley. This can be either from lack of air, or failure to watch the horizon in a rocking boat. When you start to feel a little queasy, head to the bow, feel the cool wind in your face, and watch the horizon. You will feel, at least a little, better almost instantly.
- **Puke overboard.** If all else fails, and you've got to hurl, do so over the side or the back of the boat. Why the side or the back? Well the bow is a bad choice, which you will regret

immediately. And the bathroom, while giving you the illusion of privacy during your tender time, is actually a trap. Once that bathroom fills up with pukey smell, you're a goner.

Chapter 5: Get Fishing!

Ok, now we got through all the details of who, what, where, and why: let's address the most important question – HOW. Offshore fishing appears deceptively simple. At its most basic, the boat takes you there, the captain finds the fish, the deckhands queue up some bait for you, and all you have to do to is drop it in. Right? Not so simple.

If you only read one chapter in this book, make this it. In this chapter I will tell you ALL my secrets for out-fishing my fellow anglers. There are really only a couple, and they are easy to master.

Basic Fishing

First let's break down the basic methods you will most commonly see on an offshore boat.

The troll

When you wake up in the morning, or whenever the boat first starts fishing, you will be trolling. The deckhands will deploy some number of lures out the back, on extremely heavy rods. Typical lures are cedar plugs or squid jigs, both of which ride through the surface foam and emulate flying fish.

Once the troll lines are deployed, the captain will call out four numbers, corresponding to the people responsible for manning those lines. **As an angler on the boat, it is your sacred duty to man the troll line when you are called.** Neglect that duty and somewhere a giant tuna dies a slow and wasteful death at the bottom of the sea.

You want to be on the troll actually, because it means while everyone else is sitting around waiting for fish to show up, YOU are fishing. That is your line out there, and if it gets bit, that's your fish. And there's really no way to screw up a troll fish once hooked. Keep tension on the line, and you will bring it in; the troll rods are typically spooled with 80 lb test.

There are days when the ONLY fish caught, come on the troll. That mainly happens during wide-open Yellowfin bites; Yellowfin are particularly susceptible to troll rigs. Albies are also suckers for cedar plugs, and yellowtail/dorado can be hooked when the boat trolls past a kelp paddy.

However, there will be days when the troll sucks. I have rarely, if ever, seen a Bluefin taken by troll. So days with lots of Bluefin, trolling becomes a chore. **Nevertheless, it is your duty to man the troll line**. When the boat stops on a kelp paddy, or a school of fish, the troll lines begin to sink. If people hook fish and the troll lines are still out, they create instant tangles. Trust me that when you hook your tuna and get wrapped around an untended troll line, you will be pissed. And trust me when I say it will happen. People routinely neglect their troll duties and it's maddening. Don't be that guy!

On days when the troll is good, you end up actually trolling very little. Every time the boat gets a 'jig strike', the captain will call for new trollers when he starts moving again. On good days you troll for 15-20 minutes, catch a bunch of fish, then chill until it's your turn again. Be sure to yell HOOK UP, or JIG STRIKE when your line gets bit.

On bad days the troll can last uncomfortably long. Sometimes it almost seems the captain falls asleep and forgets to rotate the numbers. Nevertheless, it is your duty: so man the troll!

....

I will share a story of heartbreak and neglect on the troll. I once took a late season charter that was completely packed. The bite was dying off for the year, and it was also a rough day at sea. Only twelve fish were caught that day, total. Twelve tuna for over 30 anglers.

My friend, and first time fisherman, Rick had come along to see what offshore fishing was about. He was the keenest new fisherman I've ever seen. Throughout the day, as he noticed people neglecting their troll duties, he would step in to man the troll for them. In fact barely a troll shift went by, that he wasn't filling in for someone. And mind you, this was a day when not a single fish came on the jig.

Fast forward to the end of the day. Everyone on the boat was completely demoralized by the sucky fishing, including me. At each grueling stop, Rick was reeling in *all 4* troll lines while everyone was trying to throw baits at the paddy. On the final stop of the day, Rick was reeling in the 4th and final troll line. For whatever reason: on that line, on that day, karma decided to pay Rick back. A tuna hit the jig while he was reeling it up from the deep. A big tuna, and he ended the day with a really nice fish.

The lesson of course, and in case I forgot to mention it: **Always man the troll when it's your time.** And be a good angler and reel one in, if you see it hanging; the fishing gods may reward you.

Finding the fish

As the boat trolls, the captain and the deckhands are constantly on the hunt for fish. When they find the fish, you'll hear the boat rev down (or sometime up first), and then it will stop to fish. Troll lines must be reeled in, and then everyone can drop baits in.

As I mentioned, the ocean is a vast blue desert; how then, does one find fish in such infinity? There are a handful of telltale signs of fish. The captain and deckhands will often sit in an elevated crow's nest, looking through gyroscopically stabilized binoculars, for one of the following:

- **Porpoises.** Tuna often work in cooperation with other predators. In fact they sometimes travel along with pods of dolphins, because their hunting techniques are complementary. Dolphins are able to herd schools of baitfish into tight balls, and the tuna move in to wreak havoc. Porpoises, especially those that are feeding, make distinct splashes on the surface of the ocean, which can be seen from quite far away.
- **Bird schools.** As with dolphins, tuna also sometimes hunt in conjunction with birds. Diving birds such as kites and terns will dive bomb the water, picking off baitfish trapped against the surface. Tuna push the bait up, and birds push them back down. Birds are one of the easiest signs, because they circle high above the school of fish. On a boat you're at sea level, and at sea level the horizon is about 3 miles away. If the observer, or the object observed, is elevated to a mere 100 ft, that distance is increased to 12 miles. Of course you can't see small birds at 12 miles, but with good binos, and a clever eye, you can see them from a helluva distance.
- **Kelp paddies.** Kelp is the oasis in the blue desert. Small fish and insects gravitate to it. Medium sized (bait) fish congregate to eat the kelp and insects, and to seek protection; a sardine in open water is a dead duck. Big fish like tuna, dorado, and yellowtail hunt around kelp, hoping to pick off any baitfish that stray too far. In short: kelp is an ecosystem. And it can be easy to see on a clear day: a huge brown mass against a field of blue.
- **Meter marks.** The boat you are on, if it's any good, will also sport an array of sophisticated electronics. Those include sonar fish finders that look below, ahead, and to the sides of the boat. Captains can often spot fish

on the meter way in the distance, and will turn the boat or speed up to get there. Meter marks can be confusing, because when the boat changes course, everyone starts looking for kelp, birds, or dolphin; but there is nothing for the angler to see.

Drift fishing

Once the boat stops, be ready to fish. Now you are into the most common form of offshore angling: drift fishing. The basic process goes like this:

1. Grab a bait from the tank.
2. Put him on the hook (nose is the most common, dorsal fin second most, anal fin third – beginners should use a nose hook).
3. Put your thumb on the spool, disengage the reel, and drop the bait in water –letting off the spool for a moment to let the line fall.
4. Apply *gentle* pressure on the (open) spool with your thumb, and slowly let the bait take line out, until you get a bite or it's time to change the bait.

This style of fishing is also called fly-lining. That's when you are connected directly to your bait and letting line out. There's a little bit of skill to this, because you want the bait to be able to swim freely (and look natural), but you don't want every surge of the bait, or boat, to set your reel spinning out of control and into a rat's nest. So apply gentle pressure, giving the bait just a little to swim against. If he's not taking line, let off with your thumb. If when the boat surges your reel spins a few extra times, apply a bit more pressure.

That's it. Sounds simple right. You'd be surprised how many people screw it up. In fact you probably will too, the first time or two. But now an important question: *Which side of the boat should you fish?*

When the boat stops, its momentum carries it forward for another minute or so. The boat is still moving forward, even with the motor in neutral. Then momentum fails, and the boat starts to catch, and turn parallel to, whatever prevailing wind is blowing. The wind is blowing the boat away.

Which side of the boat should you fish?

Ask yourself: if the boat is moving away from the wind, and you are dropping a bait and letting line out, and everyone else is dropping a bait, which side of the boat should you fish? On the leeward side, the bait will immediately be sucked under, rubbed against the keel, and left to do whatever on the windward side of the boat. On the windward side, the bait will be carried out to sea, or rather, you will drift away from it. Which of those sounds most desirable?

Hopefully it is clear: if you are fishing a bait you **must** fish on the windward side of the boat. As the boat drifts away from the bait, and you gently let it take line out, there is a straight line (literally, of nylon) from you to your bait. This is how 30+ people can fish baits on a boat and not get tangled. Everyone has a straight fishing line between them and their bait as the boat drifts away. This is called staying tight to your bait.

It is incredibly easy to get confused about this, and every drift is different, and there are always lots of people doing it wrong. But fortunately there is an easy rhyme to remember when bait fishing: ***If the wind's in your face, you're in the right place.***

I have been offshore fishing for over ten years, have caught so many fish, and am the author of a famous tuna fishing book. So you may be surprised to learn that *every time I drop a bait, I first check if the wind is in my face.* You should too.

There is, however, another little wrinkle to this method. Boats rarely drift evenly in the wind. Usually they slide slowly forward in addition to sideways. So that if you are on the correct side, with your line tight, after short while it will not be straight out ahead of you but usually diagonally slanted toward the stern.

This brings up the second rule of drift fishing: ***Follow your bait.*** You don't really need to know how a boat drifts, you are running the experiment minute-by-minute. If your line is tight, but slanted to the left, take a couple steps to the left until it's straight out again. In fact, you basically have to keep moving, slowly, the whole time in order to keep that line straight out ahead of you.

It maybe sounds like a lot of work, but after a few drifts you will start to get the hang of it. And remember, it's for your own good as well as everyone else's. There is a good deal of competition on boats, but one of my favorite deckhands always says, "We are a tuna fishing team. We will all catch more fish if we follow our lines and work together." In competition on boats, everyone loses.

Sorry, but there's just one more complication, that I'm really hard pressed to explain. But I can tell you it happens and how to avoid it. If we are all fishing and following our baits, that typically means the best thing is to start from the bow (if the boat drifts forward) and follow the bait all the way to the stern, and then reel in, change baits, and start over. For some reason, some people always start on the stern. And as the boat drifts, they end up following their baits in the opposite direction to you. Really the boat is drifting forward and sideways, so the back corner is a sort of nexus of fisherman.

So even though you followed my advice: started at the bow, wind in your face, and followed your bait all the way to the stern, now you meet some ass-hat in the back corner, stepping the other way, and telling YOU to follow your bait.

This, my friends, is the eternal misunderstanding between fishermen. You cannot solve it. Your best bet is to reel in, change baits, and head to the bow to start over.

Fishing a live bait is really the most exciting part about offshore angling. As the boat surges in the waves, you will feel little runs from your bait. Sometimes that really is the bait making a little dash. More often it's the boat falling down a wave crest, and the drag of all that line in the water pulling more out.

You will be tempted to think these little surges are something happening. Most often they are not. What you are looking for is a real run of your bait. Sometimes your bait will sense its impending doom, and make a run for it. You will feel a good little surge, more than 1 second long.

But what you are really waiting for is a tuna to pick up that bait and rocket away with it. So when you feel the line running out, your heart will skip a beat, but you have to wait a sec. In fact you have to wait 3-5.

When you really have a fish on, you will know. That line will start peeling off, and accelerating. Let him run with the bait. Count to three or five, engage the reel, and lift your rod tip up to 45 degrees. No need to do a crazy bass-fisherman hook set; the fish's own momentum will set the hook. Now you're tight to a fish!

....

Of course everything I've said is backwards if you're fishing a lure (covered below). Because you will be casting out and quickly retrieving, you can fish from anywhere on the boat. So I will pose the question to you: *Which side of the boat should you fish?*

You could, of course, fish from anywhere. However your choices are: a) the windward side of the boat, choked with bait fisherman, b) the bow, where all bait fisherman are going to start their drift, c) the stern, where a bunch of ass-clowns are all tangled up, or d) the leeward side of the boat, where *no one* is fishing.

Yes, as a lure fisherman you could fish anywhere. But the courteous thing is to fish the leeward side. Believe me, it's better for everyone, especially you.

Live bait

Sardines chillin in the bait tank.

Now a note on baits. I told you this was the most important chapter of the book. I will let you in on a little secret: this is the most important section, of the most important chapter, of this book.

Yes, ladies and gentlemen, without further ado, here is the real secret to my offshore angling success. You might not understand it. You might not believe it. But here it is. Are you ready? Here it is:

Choose a good bait.

That's it. Really. And you would be surprised how many people I've shown, let alone tried to tell; but no one wants to listen. But now that I've given up this little secret, perhaps you will indulge in hearing its history.

I began offshore fishing with family, and soon after, with a coworker and buddy named Tom. Tom often out-fished me, and on one particularly hard trip, where most fish came off the troll, Tom had hooked several fish on bait when I had hooked none.

I had some fish to take home, thanks to the productive troll. But I asked Tom, "What's your secret?" He shrugged, but asked me, "Are you handling your baits real gentle? Did you wash the sunscreen off your hand?" (many anglers believe fish can smell or taste sunscreen, and avoid it at all costs.)

Tom's questions got me thinking, but I didn't quite make the connection. On the trip I mentioned above, with Rick and the troll fish, where only twelve fish total were caught, I had another chance to learn.

It is easy to think that with 30+ anglers on a boat, all dropping baits over the side, that luck pretty much takes it from there. Right? I mean, 30 or 40 sardines in the water, and maybe 100-1000 tuna; any or all those baits could get hit. Even if there was only one feeding tuna in the water; theoretically all baits have an equal probability right?

Wrong.

On that fated twelve fish trip (on which, incidentally, I got skunked) one guy caught three tuna. Now I'm a scientist. I simply cannot accept that if every one of 30+ anglers has an equal chance of hooking a fish, one guy could catch three out of twelve.

So I went to the guy (and he had a scary Patriots neck tattoo), and I asked him, "What's your secret." He too shrugged, but at least he replied, "Choose a good bait."

Well the offseason for tuna fishing is long; basically 11 months. I thought long and hard about his advice. I realized, I had been thinking that with 40 baits in the water, there was equal probability that tuna could choose any one.

But I realized that logic was backwards. With 40 baits in the water, why wouldn't the tuna choose the best one? I had a missing piece of the puzzle. And on my next trip, I asked the (rare female) deckhand how to choose a bait.

Now recall that I told you a deckhand knows 1000x more than you will ever know about fishing. That was a lie because the factor is actually much closer to 1 million.

This particular lady gave me a doctoral thesis on choosing a bait that would be difficult to reproduce in print. But the highlights were:

- It should have all its scales
- It should not be bloody at all, especially in the nose and face
- It should be difficult to corral in the bait hand-tank
- It should be as lively as possible

Those are all excellent criteria, which I always use when choosing a bait. I can only add that I use an empirical test to determine whether I have chosen wisely or not. As they say, the proof of the pudding is in the eating.

Here's the test: when I drop that bait in the water he better swim away from the boat like a bat out of hell. He better take off like a goddamn rocket ship. He should behave as though he were a tiny baitfish, trapped aboard a ship full of demented lunatics, all prepared to jam a hook through his face and feed him to large predators.

But I digress. It is normal for a bait to exhibit, temporarily, a condition I like to call boat shock. When you drop a bait in the water, it will almost inevitably swim in circles while it gathers its bearing. This can usually be corrected by reeling in enough line until the bait just starts to come out the water, and then do a little mini-cast, underhand, to get him 5-10 feet away from the boat.

If the bait doesn't rocket out right away, or after a correction, he's dead to me. I real him in, unhook him, toss him out as chum, and go get another one. Make no mistake, this sounds simple but it is disheartening to start fishing and stop immediately. It is also a challenging obstacle course to get back to the bait tank, in the stern, and then return to the bow.

I think these challenges prevent most people from fishing a good bait. That, or an over-weaning sense of protection of one's bait. But I tell you: I will often change baits 5-10 times before I find one I like.

It is a pain in the ass, but my method speaks for itself. I've been on trips where every swimmy bait gets picked up, it's insane. And since I've discovered this method, I can't remember a trip where anyone caught more fish than I did.

Kelp Paddies

A note on kelp: When the boat finds kelp it will pull over and everyone will drift fish by it. The thing to understand is that kelp is not a target; it's an ecosystem. You don't need to cast your bait right at or into the kelp, and you really don't need to have the first bait in the water.

There are fish in a 100 yard circle or more around that kelp. In fact the biggest fish often hang out in the fringes of the kelps circle of influence. So don't fret that you can't see the kelp, or it's on the wrong side of the boat, or someone got a bait in before you. Fish the kelp with a lively bait and some patience, and you will be rewarded.

Advanced Fishing Topics

If you can stand by your troll line and fly-line a sardine, you are 90% of the way to catching your first tuna. Choose a good bait, fish with the wind in your face, follow your bait, and you will find that Robert is your father's brother.

However there are a few tactics below that will earn you extra fish. You can use these on days when the troll is a droll, or when only yellows are hitting the sardines. You can also use them to get away from crowds, or mix up your fishing experience once you get good at fly lining.

The slide

The slide is a deadly secret that many people have heard of, but practically no one uses. That's partly because it requires a little dedication.

It relies on the moment of confusion that occurs, both above deck and below, when a jig strike occurs. When the boat is trolling, it will sometimes run over a school of fish (hopefully by design). The lures trolled out the back appear to be flying fish, surfing the wake of the boat. This set-up will dupe tuna into biting an otherwise lifeless cylinder; a common troll lure is a simple rod of cedar.

In the ideal case, when one or more troll lines get bit (and indeed, sometimes 2, 3, or even 4 will get bit at the same time). The boat stops immediately and the deckhands begin throwing baitfish into the water: chumming. The goal is to get the school to follow their hooked brethren up to the boat, whereupon, everyone gets chance to catch one.

When that happens it's an amazing, frenetic mess. Tuna begin leaping out of the water all around the boat, eating the baitfish. It's a feeding frenzy that is a sight to behold. And usually everyone gets bit right away; which comes with its own mess of tangled lines.

This frenzy can last sometimes for hours, or a few brief minutes. But more often, one or two fish are hooked and the rest of the school high-tails it out of there; spooked by the boat or the hooked fish.

The slide is a method that capitalizes on the brief confusion of the tuna school below you, and the relative calm of the fisherman around you. The goal is to put a bait in a tuna's face immediately upon a jig strike, before the school scatters. Here's how you do it:

Rig a swimbait, on a heavy jig head (1-2 oz), onto one of your rigs. Use a medium to heavy rig for this, both because the fish will not have a lot of time to stare at your fishing line, and you are likely to hook a fish while the boat is still moving; that will put more tension on your line.

With your swim bait rigged, move to the back corner of the boat and stand ready. When the boat eventually stops, it will make a little arc in the first instants of its drift. If you can contrive to be on the outside corner of the arc, all the better. Standing in the corner, be ready to drop that swimbait into the drink. I usually have the bail open with my thumb on the reel so all I have to do is let it go.

The INSTANT someone yells 'HOOK-UP'. Lift your thumb to drop the bait, and then apply just the teeniest amount of pressure for controlled line release. Your swimbait will fall down and back in the water; hopefully right into the school of fish you just passed. Count to 30 or so, then engage the reel and reel up as quickly as possible.

This method is called the slide, because you are sliding a bait down to the school of fish. The boat moves past the school, as everyone is grabbing a bait, and the trollers are reeling in. But your little swimbait is essentially sea-anchored at the site of the fish. It will sink through them, and often get bit on the way down. Or sometimes the sudden dash to the surface will trigger a bite.

If you don't get bit that first time, stow that rod and fish a bait. But keep trying; I have caught tuna on the slide on days when only yellowtails were biting. After that everyone wants to fish the slide.

But in general no one does. I think that's because no one wants to stand in the back corner all day waiting to drop a bait. But here's another secret: you don't necessarily have to wait all day. I usually only stand at the ready when: A) there are lots of jig strikes, and I don't have to wait long, or B) when the boat changes rpms or makes a turn – that usually indicates the captain has seen something, and a jig strike might be imminent.

Chucking iron

Chucking iron is a generic term for casting a lure. If you are fishing a proper bait caster reel, on a stout rod, casting will be hard. If you set up a jig stick, with a longer, springier rod, you will have a better chance.

Bear in mind that you will also have to manage the reel differently. Place your thumb on the reel, disengage the reel, and swing back and then forward in one motion. Don't try to 'spring' the bait out there so much as swing it. This isn't the bass rod you're used to fishing, and you don't have nearly as much give.

Once the bait is flying in front of you, lift your thumb off the reel and let the line fly. When the lure is just about to hit the water, put your thumb back on the reel quickly, and then engage the reel and work your lure. If the bait hits the water before you've thumbed the reel, the spool will keep spinning and pile the line up into a huge tangle.

In bait casting, as in life, timing is everything. So start slow, and maybe practice in the backyard to get your timing down.

But once you can cast, there is no limit to the lures you can fish. Casting and retrieving swimbaits is a popular choice, especially if you are already rigged to fish the slide.

Surface irons are another popular choice. They look kind of like long Madeleine cookies but are made of ceramic type composite. They're designed for a fast cast and retrieve, so that they flutter along the surface.

Yoyo jigs are fished like their eponymous toy. You let them sink for a while, sometimes very deep if you are fishing for yellowtail around islands, and then jig them up and down (or reel, sink, reel).

There are a variety of spoon type baits; curved metal lures that are shiny on one side. Those can be reeled quickly through the surface film, cast and retrieved slowly, or even yoyo-ed.

Some people will even fish surface poppers when a bite is really good.

The Fight

Reeling

Once you've hooked a tuna, or any offshore fish, you're in for a fight! Even if you've caught large fish in fresh water, you will be surprised how strong ocean fish are. Even a 10-15 lb fish, living in open water, will outfight any freshwater fish you've caught.

If you have fished freshwater, you know you need to keep your rod up, and tension on the line. Because these fish are heavier and stronger, you will most likely not be able to maintain the 45 degree angle on the rod for the whole fight. When your fish is far from the boat, keep the rod up. But as he comes closer, and swims directly down, you will have your rod pretty much horizontal over the rail.

In either case, maintain focus while fighting the fish. Keep tension on the line at all times. You will have to lift the rod up gently, and then *carefully* reel down to the fish, always maintaining tension. Don't pump; rather, lift up and reel down - slowly. A common mistake is to lift the rod, then lower it too quickly while reeling, creating a momentary ease in line tension. At all times move cautiously and deliberately.

A clever trick is to use the boat to help you fight your fish. The boat will surge upward in the waves and then ease gently back down. Keep tension on the way up, and reel on the way down. That saves some effort from your forearms. And when the rod is horizontal, you can even rest it, at the handle, on the rail. DO NOT rest any of the fiberglass portion of your rod on the rail because that circumvents the spring of the rod, and will often to lead to breakage.

One last thing on reeling. Most tuna reels have a completely open spool; there is no line guiding system like you have, inherently, on a spinning reel. If you simply reel in a bunch of line, it will invariably pile up on one side of the spool. So as you reel, you will have to use the thumb of the hand holding the rod, to guide the line back and forth so it feeds nicely back onto the reel. That's where the waterproof finger tape is nice, it helps prevent line burn/cuts.

That is hard to do the first few hundred times you are reeling in a bait casting reel. It is especially hard to remember, and execute, when you have the weight and excitement of a fish on the line. But with practice you will get it. Just tie some heavy lead on the line and practice casting and reeling in the backyard, you will get the feel for it.

Landing

As you fight your fish, he will make at least several sounds to the deep. The first few will be big runs, sometimes lasting 10-30s.

These are scary because the fish seems strong and the reel seems tiny.

But as he pulls line out, he increases the drag he experiences. The line in the water is additional drag. And as your line runs out, he has to turn a smaller radius on your spool; he loses torque. Rest assured you will almost never run out of line, unless you've hooked something extremely large; like a marlin or a seal. Remain calm and wait for him to finish his run before you start reeling again.

As the fight progresses, the runs will be shorter and shorter. Eventually the fish will tire and will only be able to just resist you pulling him in. That's when your arms are burning and your back is aching. But keep reeling, you're almost there.

By the time the fish is tired, he is pretty much directly beneath the boat. So you will be leaning out over the rail a bit, and the rod will be horizontal. As he starts to come up, you will see the first glint of light of his iridescent skin. At that point, feel free to say/yell "deep color!" This indicates to the deck hands you have glimpsed the fish, and he will probably be up in the next few minutes.

As the fish comes up even closer to the surface, you will get your first good look at him. He will usually turn on his side for a second, before making his final dive; which will be bigger than the last few half-hearted attempts. The sight of the boat usually gives the fish a second wind for the fight. In any case, when you get that full glimpse, call out "color!" That lets the deckhands know that you will be calling for the gaff soon.

Finally your fish will give up the fight. He will turn on his side and start doing 'death circles' at the surface. As you continue to reel in, those circles will get tighter. At this point it's critical to keep the fish calm and circling. Remain calm yourself and make sure you keep his head in the water, even pitching down if you have to, when the boat surges up.

When the fish is in his death spiral, it's time to call the deckhands over. Just yell "GAFF!" as loud as you can and they will come running. Chances are, if you yelled "color" a few seconds ago, he's already there.

Now is the key timing part, which separates pro fisherman and deckhands from hacks. This is a dance between you two and the fish. As the fish is circling, and heading right for his point of closest approach to the boat, take one step backward and lower your rod tip slightly (to keep the fish's head down).

You are not trying to pull the fish in closer, he will circle in himself. You are trying to create a predictable trajectory for the fish and move out of the deckhand's way at the critical moment. The fish will continue his little circle, and the deckhand will be able to time his gaff perfectly.

If you get your timing right, the deckhand will nail the fish right in the head, preserving all that sushi-grade fish you worked so hard to get. If you screw up, you'll probably get a meat gaff, and will have to throw out some of your precious sushi.

Lastly, and extremely important: as the deckhand brings your fish over the rail, place you thumb on the spool and disengage the reel. A sharp hook, connected to a strong spring, can be a deadly implement. If anything goes wrong (fish jumps off the gaff, deckhand trips, etc) you want line to peel off your reel, rather than have a hook flying back at you or stuck in someone's flesh. Open up your reel!

Drag setting

If you rented your rod, they have probably set the drag for you. But before I drop a bait in the water I always check my drag. I like to use line that is stronger than my drag, so that line tension will always be less than line strength. For example, the Shimano Torium 20 reel can apply a maximum of 20lb of drag, and I always spool with 25 lb line or heavier.

When you are getting ready to fish, make one loop of line around your hand (don't just grab it) and pull some line out against the drag. If you can just pull it out, without cutting your hand off, you are set about right; approximately 10-15 lb.

Once you hook a fish, you can always adjust; but do so with caution! If a fish is constantly taking line out, or if when I crank the handle no line comes in (reeling against the drag), I will tighten it ONE CLICK. Later, if I'm still losing too much ground, I might go another click, and so on. But never move more than one click at a time, without some checking in between.

Likewise if the fish is trying to run but no line comes out of the reel, I might even loosen the drag, both to prolong the experience and to make sure I'm not stressing my line too much. In general it is better to be a bit light on the drag.

Once your fishing trip is over, and especially when your fishing season is over, completely loosen all drags on your reels. Storing reels with their drags set is the best way to ruin drag systems. They work by compressing a friction ring inside, and if left in the compressed state for too long, it loses its effectiveness.

Terminology

While you are fishing, here are some key terms you might hear screamed across the boat:

- Hook Up! – normally yelled at the top of your lungs when you get a bite
- Fresh One! – Also yelled, this is your way to let the crew/captain know that you have a new bite, in the midst of heavy action

- Deep Color – as your fish comes up to the surface, you will see the glint of light off his side. This terms lets deckhands know you have a fish coming up
- Color! – when your fish is very close to the surface
- Gaff! – means your fish is lolling on his side at the surface, and you need a deckhand to come pull it over the rail with a giant hook on a pole.

Key Fishing Concepts Summary

This book is starting to run quite long. In case your brain is falling asleep, here are the key concepts of this chapter.

- **Always man your troll line**
- **Wind in your face, you're in the right place**
- **Follow your bait**
- **Choose a good bait**

Chapter 6: Handling the Catch

When you're packing for your tuna trip, don't forget to bring the most important piece of gear: a cooler. You're bringing home some Grade A tuna here. Sushi grade Ahi. You've gone to the all the trouble of getting it, so handle it carefully, and it will feed you for a long time.

Proper handling of the catch begins at the gaff. Fish starts to spoil the instant blood stops flowing. Good boats will bleed the fish right away, and great boats will then throw it into the refrigerated salt water tank. RSW is great because it can keep your fish below 32F, without quite freezing it. Whole fish, kept at low temp, can stay fresh for a long time.

Fish Cleaning

On most boats, the deckhands will offer to clean your fish; for a fee. They will completely break down the fish for you; or you can have them just remove the head and guts; or you can choose to take the whole fish home and do it yourself.

The choice is not easy. It is tempting to do the work yourself; after all, you went out there and caught it, why not do your own butchery. Also, keeping the fish whole keeps them fresh longer. When the meat is exposed to air and/or rinsed with water, it is contaminated with bacteria, which will eventually spoil it.

On the other hand, these fish are big, sometimes really, really big. Unless you have a giant cooler, and some friends to help you carry it out to your car, you're going to have your hands full.

I always have my fish cleaned on the boat, but I always feel kind of bad about not doing it myself. On the other hand, the deckhands make most of their money from cleaning fish, so it's nice to let them make a few bucks.

The laws regarding cleaning fish on boats change yearly. At present, in California, the collar and belly must be kept together. The loins can be cut off the carcass, but must be kept whole, and the all the meat, head, and belly must go in one bag. The going rate for this service is $7 per fish.

When I have my fish cleaned on the boat, I ask them to leave the skin on; it doesn't matter what kind of fish it is. The skin will act as a protective barrier against air, water, bacteria, etc; it will keep your fish that much fresher.

Whether you have your fish cleaned on the boat or not, don't miss the chance to watch. First all the fish from the whole trip are brought back up on deck, and sorted by number. (You remember your number right?). Then people are allowed to pose for photos with their fish, and generally chaos ensues.

On good trips, the boat will have caught its limit. The boat limit is the number of anglers multiplied by the max fish per angler. So it is legal for you to catch more than your limit, as long as the boat is under its limit. If you have surplus fish, at the time of fish sorting they will allocate some of your fish to others who were not so lucky. If you're fast with the stapler, you can even get in there and make sure your buddies are the ones who get your extra fish.

The deckhands will then put out a huge plank of wood and commence the best fish fillet factory show you've ever seen.

Each loin (or pair of loins, if it's a small fish) will be rinsed in the bait tank (salt water) and then go into a gallon ziplock bag. The collar and belly will go in a gallon or trash bag, and all those bags will go in a big blue trash bag. That's for each fish. Finally, all your individual blue fish bags will go into another set of blue trash bags, and then back into the RSW for the rest of the trip home.

On a good day you will be walking down the docks with 2-3 really heavy, really slimy and gross, blue trash bags. As I mentioned, having a buddy to help shuttle vehicles makes this process considerably easier.

You have a huge cooler in the car right? You can usually buy ice right at the dock. But if not there is invariably a gas station or grocery store nearby where you can get some. The RSW leaves the fish nearly frozen, but it is important to get that fish back on ice ASAP, and keep it on ice until it's consumed.

Let me repeat that: *Don't be lazy or casual with your fish, keep it on ice at all times from now on.*

Processing and Storage

Whenever I go offshore fishing, I also dedicate the next day to processing the fish. "What is there to process?" you might ask. "Isn't the fish already cut up?"

Did you notice above where I said all your fish will be rinsed in the bait tank? Gross right? The water in the bait tank is pumped in from the ocean, and back out, but after the first fish or two is it pretty much stained blood red. That bloody bait tank water is not doing your fish any favors. It is literally a stew of bacterial contamination that will rapidly spoil your fish. The sooner you address your fish, and the better you handle it from there, the better it will be.

The goal here is to take all your fish out of the dirty cooler, clean it up, portion it out, wrap it up tight, and store it back in a clean cooler. Here's what you need to get started:

- Your dirty cooler filled with the slimy/bloody ice and all your blue bags of fish.
- A very sharp knife and a sharpening stone.
- A box of gallon zip-lock bags and saran wrap or vacuum sealer bags

- A roll of paper towels.
- A nice big, clean work area, preferably in a cool place (it is summer) and near running water. But be prepared to get this workspace completely covered in fish slime and blood. I usually clear off one whole counter top in my kitchen.
- A large plastic cutting board, with something underneath to keep it from sliding around; a piece of the rubber, gridded, shelf padding works great.
- A clean cooler filled with clean ice. Another option is to use a large bowl, with some ice in the bottom, in the refrigerator.

Once you're set up, cut open all the blue bags, releasing the gallon ziplock bags inside. Make a mental survey of how many loins you have and sort them by the ones that look the best (generally, redder is better). Try to keep the fish on ice as much as possible, just shifting it around in the cooler. Then ask yourself a hard question: *How much fish can I realistically eat in the next 4 days?*

When I'm sorting, I place the fish into one of the following groups:

- Premium stuff to be eaten raw over the next 2-3 days.
- Premium to great stuff to be eaten seared over the next 3-4 days.
- Premium to great stuff to be given away to friends and family, and eaten within 3-4 days.
- Great to good looking stuff that can be vacuum sealed and frozen, and eaten cooked over the next 1-2 months.
- Trimmings and good or lesser quality to be smoked immediately, vacuum sealed, frozen, and eaten over the rest of the year.

In all cases, air and moisture are the enemies, so always work clean, wipe surfaces and fish dry, and either vacuum seal the fish (yes even the fish you will eat tomorrow) or wrap it as tightly as possible in saran wrap and then place in a gallon bag (as a leak guard) as you go. You're going to use a lot of plastic bags and paper towels here, just get used to it.

Once you have a general idea of where the fish is going, the process is simple:

1. Lift a gallon bag to the board, pull out a loin, and replace the bag in the cooler
2. Wipe down the loin clean, on all exposed sides with a paper towel (never rinse!)
3. Fillet the meat off the skin and then move the meat to a clean portion of the board.
4. Throw away the skin, wipe down the board
5. Wipe the fish clean on all sides with clean paper towels, cut it to portion, and then
    a. If the fish is going to be eaten fresh: vacuum seal and place back on ice
    b. If the fish is going to be frozen, vacuum seal and put in the freezer.
    c. If the fish is going to the smoker, place in a gallon ziplock bag (use a new/clean bag, but feel free to fill it up.
6. Wipe down the board, touch up your knife edge, and repeat until all the fish is processed.

Again, I want to stress: Keep your fish on ice, and stored airtight, as much as humanly possible. Keep all surfaces clean and dry. Properly handled cuts will remain tasty and fresh for at least 4 days, possibly more.

Cooking and eating

Now for the part you've all been waiting for; time to chow down.

Raw Fish

Tuna spend their whole life at sea, in deep, open salt water. There are few parasites that live in that environment and few opportunities to spread parasites among individual fish. It is rare to even find parasites on pelagic fish. And they are sufficiently biologically different from us that there is very little risk of a saltwater fish parasite infecting you.

However there are upwards of several cases each year, of people getting sick from eating raw fish. Be warned. But know that many fisherman, including this one, not only eat their catch raw, but relish the chance.

You will never have sushi as fresh as that which you caught yourself. Simply sliced thin and served with soy and wasabi it is delicious. Or if you're feeling adventurous, go the Italian way – crudo. Juice a bit of lemon onto a plate, arrange the sliced fish on top, and then drizzle high quality olive oil, and salt and pepper over. Raw is seriously the superior way to eat fresh fish.

I will quite happily eat raw tuna and yellowtail for the first few days after I've brought it home. I am meticulous about keeping everything clean, airtight, and cold. As it starts to age, even in ideal conditions, its starts to exhibit a subtle rainbow pattern across a cut edge. Once I see the rainbow (and you can't miss it) I stop eating it raw.

Poke

Poke is another raw application, invented by Hawaiians. It's fantastic. There are literally thousands of poke recipes out there, but many of them share some common ground: salt, soy sauce, sesame oil, chives, onions, and sesame seeds.

I have made poke a few times, and honestly, I never tracked the ingredients. I usually start with 1-2 lb of chunked fish and add a few healthy dashes of oil, a few pinches of salt, soy sauce, and about ¼ of a sweet onion and/or ¼ cup chives, then mix, taste, and adjust. Spread the sesame seeds over the top once you like the flavors, and let it cure for at least an hour in the fridge. The salt and soy sauce will make the fish extra firm, and delicious.

Searing

Whether to please picky eaters, to get some variety, or because it's been sitting around for more than 2 days and getting the rainbow pattern, your fresh tuna will be excellent seared. That means cooking the outside of the fish hot and fast, but leaving the inside raw.

Searing the fish preserves the really nice quality that fresh, raw fish can give to a meal. I will sear fish that's been sitting on ice for more than 3 days (but less than 5-6). I will also thaw some of the premium stuff I froze and eat it seared for the first couple of weeks after a trip. Generally as long as it smells good to me, I sear it.

The key to searing is an extreme heat and a little prep of the fish. A very hot pan or a very hot grill are key. Make sure you have oil on the fish, and if grilling, oil the grill itself.

Cut the fish so that it has flat sides running lengthwise. Usually that will mean a square or triangular cross section. Place the fish on the hot pan or grill and don't walk away. Some people count to 30. I just watch as the cooked part of the fish creeps up from the pan. As the fish cooks it turns opal-white. So when I see approximately ¼" of whitish flesh creeping up the side, I turn the fish. Sear all sides, or if you want to get fancy, sear two opposing sides of a square and leave the other sides raw.

As for flavor, there are a lot of possibilities. Olive oil, salt, and pepper are a classic combination, which really highlight the natural flavor of the fish cooked that way. Yellowfin and Bluefin have a bright flavor; almost like you added lemon juice, but you haven't.

Tropical and Asian flavors compliment seared tuna as well. Think ginger, passion fruit, pineapple, soy, sesame oil. Either as marinades or as a glaze, any (or all) of these are delicious on fish.

I have never tried to reproduce it, but a restaurant I used to frequent served a seared Yellowfin, crusted with pepper, coriander, and a bit of sugar; I'd swear I was eating the most tender fillet mignon ever.

Cooking fish

If the fish has been vacuum sealed and frozen for more than 3-4 weeks, it generally starts to lose some of its quality. At that point I go with stronger marinade and cook to at least medium. For no particular reason, I also tend to cook the white-fleshed fishes to at least medium as well; those include yellowtail, dorado, and wahoo.

Here are a few templates which I have found work well for all cases:

- Marinate in teriyaki for a few hours and grill.
- Crust with sesame seeds and sear in sesame oil
- Crust with crushed macadamia nuts and sear in coconut oil, served with pineapple glaze
- Marinate in Moroccan marinade (recipe below) and grill until charred (delicious!)

Here are some ideas I'd like to try

- Marinate in Thai peanut sauce and grill
- Slather in passion fruit BBQ sauce and grill

Moroccan Marinade

I can't claim to have invented this recipe. It is based on one I found in Paul Johnson's *Fish Forever*. You can look up the recipe there, but I always throw it together from memory:

- ½ c of olive oil
- 1-2 T paprika
- 1-2 t salt
- 1 t fresh ground black pepper
- A chunk of preserved lemon, chopped fine
- 2-3 cloves of garlic, chopped
- 1-2 T chopped fresh mint
- 1-2 T chopped fresh cilantro
- ½ c plain yogurt (optional)

Mix it all up into a paste and rub it over chunks of tuna. Even better is when you have 1" chunks from trimming. Toss them into the marinade, mix well, and let stand 2-3 h. Then skewer and grill.

Poke and Ahi Burgers

Chances are you've had a fish sandwich somewhere in your life: usually a breaded and fried fillet, with lettuce, tomato, mayo, on a bun. If not, you should order one immediately.

It turns out that tuna makes an excellent sandwich as well, and it's much easier to prepare than all that breaded deep fried stuff. Seared ahi is a real treat between two slices of bread. Grill or fry it briefly, keeping the inside rare, and throw it on a bun you're your favorite burger toppings. Ahi burgers rule!

If the fish is not quite fresh enough to sear, consider adding some flavor and cooking it to well done. I once made poke but then didn't eat it in time. So I ground it up in the food processor, with some eggs and breadcrumbs, and made poke burgers. They were delicious too.

Bellies and collars

I am a huge proponent of using as much of the animal as possible. Deckhands used to throw all but the loins away, but we could pay extra to keep the bellies. Now California state law now requires that if the fish is filleted on a boat, the belly and the collar must go with it.

The front collarbone assembly, once removed, resembles the jaws of a shark; like what people hang on the wall. It has become fashionable recently to save and eat the collar. The collar contains a variety of flesh-types, from light meat to dark meat, some delectably oily and others a bit fishy. It also contains bones, teeth, cartilage, etc. Because the collar is so large, it's hard to do much with it other than roast or grill it.

In either case, hit it with a healthy dose of olive oil, salt, and pepper, or a strong marinade, and cook until it's a bit charred. Then scrape out any meat you can into tortillas, and top with cilantro and lime. It's worth the extra (large, ungainly) bag that you have to bring home.

Bellies are the fatty, bottom part of the fish. In fact, nearly all fish (and for that matter, creatures) store extra fat in their belly. In some freshwater fish this fatty meat is not tasty, but with tuna it can often be the best bit.

You should absolutely save the belly of any Bluefin you catch; pound for pound they have the thickest bellies. With Bluefin, the belly is actually an expensive delicacy. Fillet the meat off the skin, then flip the meat over, and do your best to fillet the meat off the somewhat thick internal membrane, and you are left with something that resembles raw fish packed together with butter. The best way to serve it is sliced thin, and raw.

Some have told me it's not worth saving the belly of small (<30lb) Yellowfin, because it's so thin; but I have always found them delicious. The simplest application is to grill them, 5-10 minutes per side, until the meat is firm and a bit charred. Then fork the meat into tortillas. Yellowfin bellies are also excellent smoked. There's no need to even brine it if you're in a hurry, just throw it on the smoker for about 1-1.5 hours, and then vacuum pack and freeze. The next time you're putting out a cheese and cracker spread, thaw the smoked belly and put it alongside; people will be amazed by how delicious it is.

Smoking fish

Smoked fish is probably my favorite invention since bread that has been run through a series of half-inch offset reciprocating serrated blades. Seriously, show me a man who doesn't love smoked fish and I will show you an utter fool. Smoking is also a great way to preserve the catch. Smoked fish, vacuum sealed and frozen, will last years without degrading in quality.

The one piece of gear you need is an electric smoker, mine cost about 50 bucks at Home Depot and looks like a red R2 unit. In fact I often fantasize about re-painting it to look like R2D2 (more often that you might think is healthy).

I screwed around first with smoking in my clamshell Weber grill, and second with a charcoal powered deal. Both turned out to be a waste of time; buy or borrow the electric one. You will also need a good smoking hard wood. I like apple or hickory, both readily available at Home Depot. Buy the big chunks not the small stuff.

I also screwed around for years with the recipe. Smoked fish has to be brined, that is, soaked in salt water. In general brining adds moisture, but in smoking it is used as a pre-cure of the meat, and helps to firm it up a bit. There are lots of recommendations (many of them nebulous) on how much salt and how much sugar to use for a given amount of water. In the end I got a tip from my friend Jarret Stevens, at Bristol Bay Salmon. Through a great deal of trial and error I have arrived at a method that is flawless. I call it the Six Twos method.

For the Six Twos, you will need 2 cups of sugar, 2 cups of salt (kosher), a 2 gallon pot, and up to 20 lb of fish. Then you will brine for 2 hours, rest for 2 hours, and smoke for 2 hours. Six Twos. This method is perfect for relatively thick fish, 2-4 inches. I have used it on salmon fillets and tuna shoulders alike. Thinner trout fillets simply require less time on the heat. A two gallon pot holds the perfect amount of fish for Smoke2D2 (another 2!).

Simple Smoked Fish

Mix the sugar and salt in a bowl (collectively, brine) and stir well. If I'm working with red-fleshed fish I use brown sugar, with white-fleshed fish I use white sugar. Here you can add herbs, pepper, citrus zest, maple syrup, or whatever you want to tweak the flavor.

Cut the fish into desired serving sizes, accounting for about 30% shrinkage. Put a thin layer of the brine into the pot. Coat all sides of a piece of fish with brine and then set in the pot. Repeat until you have a layer of fish, and then sprinkle a layer of brine over the layer, and continue. When all the fish is coated, sprinkle the excess brine over the top. Cover and refrigerate for 1 hour. After that hour is up, take the pot out, stir everything up as best you can, (trying to get the top stuff to the bottom). And put back in the fridge for another hour (2 total)

After the second hour is up, remove the pot from the fridge. A hearty sludge of sugar, salt, and gelatinous protein will have engulfed the fish. Remove each piece and rinse well, it should be much firmer at this stage. Set aside on a wire rack. I use baking racks on cookie sheets. When all the fish is racked, put the racks in the fridge for 2 hours. You can also use a cool place with a fan blowing over it.

This rest period allows the fish to form a thin skin of protein, called a pellicle. The pellicle absorbs flavor, holds moisture, and gives the whole thing a great look and texture. While the pellicle is forming start soaking 5 pieces of fist sized wood in water.

After two hours the surface of the fish should be glossy and beautiful. It should feel tacky but not sticky. Set the racks on the counter, letting the fish come to room temp. In the meantime, fill the water bowl in your smoker, plug it in, and add the soaked wood. In 15-20 minutes the smoker should be hot and wisps of fragrant smoke should be coming out. Add the fish to the racks and wait. After about 1 hour the smoke will subside; add a few more pieces of wood and keep waiting.

Somewhere between 1.5 and 2 hours the fish will be done. It goes from perfect to kind of burnt rather quickly, so after 1 hour, start checking it every 10-15 minutes. When it looks brown, dry, and delicious (not white and juicy or completely black) pull it off. Set it back on the racks to cool, and finally vacuum pack and freeze for later use.

Or consume immediately. Smoked fish makes a great fish salad (with mayo and mustard), is nice on a regular salad, and is superb on fluffy quinoa or creamy polenta.

About the Author

Matt Steiger is a physicist, writer, homebrewer, fisherman, urban farmer, forager, and fresh egg evangelist. He lives in San Diego with his wife, two kitties, a small flock of chickens, and three bee hives. He has published multiple scientific papers in peer-reviewed journals, as well as articles on farming, fishing, and fermentation for local magazines.

You can follow his misadventures at www.thefoodlunatic.com, or email him comments and erratum: steigey@gmail.com

Made in the USA
Las Vegas, NV
28 September 2022